£ 6.99

808.82 PIC

TOGETHER NOW

KEN PICKERING

DUOLOGUE SCENES FOR YOUNG PERFORMERS

DRAMATIC LINES, TWICKENHAM, ENGLAND
text copyright © Ken Pickering

This book is intended to provide resource material for speech and drama festivals, workshops, examinations and for use in schools and colleges. No permission is required for amateur performance.

Dramatic Lines
PO Box 201
Twickenham
TW2 5RQ
England

A CIP record for this book is available from the British Library

ISBN 0 9537770 1 4

Together Now first published
in 2000
by
Dramatic Lines
Twickenham   England

Printed by The Dramatic Lines Press
Twickenham England

FOREWORD

I was delighted to find that Ken Pickering had compiled this book of duologues. Sourcing suitable material for young actors is never easy, and the care he has taken in choosing this anthology makes it a boon for students and teachers alike.

On reading a selection of the pieces I was pleased to note the range and variety of styles, characters and situations. This useful resource book contains something for everyone.

The duologue offers an excellent opportunity for young performers to practise basic performance skills. Besides characterisation there are requirements for a high level of concentration, focus, eye contact and perhaps most important of all, listening skills.

I am certain that this collection will be widely used and enjoyed by students, teachers, audiences and examiners for many years to come.

Stephanie Manuel LLAM
Founder Principal Stagecoach Theatre Arts

for my friends at the
London College of Music and Media

INTRODUCTION

What we think of as 'theatre' probably began when a second actor joined a solo performer on stage. Working together to create a scene between two characters is a particularly enjoyable aspect of drama and these scenes are designed to give you a huge range of different experiences. Some are complete small plays in themselves whilst others are extracts, but you should think of each as a complete play which your audience needs to understand.

I once read a fascinating article about play writing in which the author said he was tired of reading plays about things that were not real. "Write about things you know," he said. I have tried to do just that; all of these scenes are either the result of direct experience or of some reading which has enriched my imagination. More than that, however, I have tried to find situations that most of us know about so that you can enter into them with that sense of belonging that is so important for good acting.

Every one of these scenes needs an imaginative use of space, careful listening and an ability to find the climaxes and tensions in the action. It is most important that you listen to each other before reacting and you must also create the impression that you are hearing your partner say the words for the first time. Part of the fun of working on a duologue comes from bouncing ideas off each other, so don't be afraid to experiment, to try things in many different ways and use the words as part of the action rather than something to which you add action at a later stage!

Never be in a hurry as you present these scenes: only you can control the way you spend your time in the scene, not an adjudicator or examiner or audience, so make the stage your own for the few minutes it takes to perform one of these scenes and enter totally into the situation shown. **Don't forget you have something to show!**

Ken Pickering

Ken Pickering

CONTENTS

ROBOTS

Dom and Indi are two robots. The stage space is completely empty.

DOM MOVES AROUND BUSILY WHILE INDI WATCHES

DOM: Look at me. I can move anywhere. I can turn, I can twist, I can bend, I can pick up.

INDI: You're lucky. I can't do much. I stand still all the time. I can only use my arms.

DOM: I've never met a robot like you before. ...... I thought they were all like me.

INDI: Oh no! There are all kinds of robot .... but most of them are like me, I think you'll find.

DOM: What do you mean, like you?

INDI: Industrial Robots: that's why my name is Indi, it's short for industrial. We work mainly in factories.

DOM: How boring. I should hate that. What do you make?

INDI: I help to make cars.
(DEMONSTRATING.) This arm moves across. Like this .....
and holds a panel in position, and then the other arm moves over and fixes bolts in it. I have a pointed gun attached to the end of my arm to fix the bolts. Like this, **brrrrrr.**

DOM: Is that all you do?

INDI: Yes, that's quite enough for me. Once I got the hang of it, I found I could do it over and over again. Like this. *(DEMONSTRATING.)*

DOM: You're certainly very good at it, but don't you find it monotonous, doing the same thing over and over again?

INDI: I don't think about it. It's not our job to think. It's people who get bored and want to be paid a lot of money for doing boring jobs. That's why they have robots. Anyway, we are better at those jobs.

DOM:	I'm sure we are ..... but I don't agree with what you said about thinking. I think a lot. I like thinking.
INDI:	So what kind of robot are you, then?
DOM:	Well, my name is Dom and I believe that's short for domestic.
INDI:	Domestic? What does that mean?
DOM:	I suppose it means we work at home. I can do all sorts of jobs in a home. I can lift, I can pick up things, I can make someone a cup of tea, I can wash up. I can .....
INDI:	I wouldn't like that ..... having people fussing around all the time. At least they just leave me to get on with it!
DOM:	So, who do you talk to?
INDI:	To the other robots, of course. The factory is full of them, all doing slightly different jobs.
DOM:	But always the **same** job. *(PAUSE.)* I've only just been invented, you know. Last week I appeared on television.
INDI:	Really! ...... In 'East Enders'?
DOM:	No, have you got a screw missing or something?
INDI:	They talk about 'East Enders' all the time in our factory.
DOM:	The programme was called 'Tomorrow's World'.
INDI:	'Tomorrow's World'? Why tomorrow? You are here today. Aren't you? *(PAUSE.)* What's it like being on 'telly'?
DOM:	It was great ..... except for the lights. It was so bright and hot that it made my sensors water. But I scuttled around the studio and showed everyone what I could do, in spite of the heat.
INDI:	Were they impressed?
DOM:	I think so ...... except that nobody's bought me yet!

INDI:	Anyway, why are you here?
DOM:	For the same reason as you, I suppose. Why are you here?
INDI:	I don't know, but I have an idea that we're on show in some kind of exhibition. Last week a team of people arrived suddenly without warning and removed me from the production line ..... and put me here. *(PAUSE.)* It said 'Museum of Science and Technology' on the board outside.
DOM:	Museum? Museum! I didn't notice that. A museum is where they put old-fashioned things. I've only just been invented!
INDI:	Perhaps that programme should have been called 'Yesterday's World'! Cheer up. Cheer up. Look, someone's coming to press our buttons ..... get ready to perform!
	THEY ARE BOTH PERFECTLY STILL AND THEN SUDDENLY BURST INTO LIFE

ACTING NOTES

I hope you will have a great deal of fun with this scene experimenting with different voices and movements to represent the two robots. Don't forget that there is a considerable contrast between them.

3

YOU TELL HER

Two young people are discussing an awkward situation. The scene can take place almost anywhere. The stage may have a couple of chairs set.

ALEX:	You tell her.
LES:	I can't.
ALEX:	Why not?
LES:	It's ..... difficult. I ......
ALEX:	Why is it so difficult?
LES:	Look, Alex, you know perfectly well why it's difficult for me.
ALEX:	I don't see why it should be.
LES:	It's very awkward. It's, ... you know.
ALEX:	What do I know?
LES:	It's an embarrassing situation.
ALEX:	No more for you than it would be for me.
LES:	So you tell her, then.
ALEX:	I've already explained why I can't do that.
LES:	Well, I'm not convinced.
ALEX:	That's not fair: you said you understood. One of us has got to tell her.
LES:	How do you suggest we do it?
ALEX:	Simple, you go up to her and say, "I've got something I need to tell you." and she'll be interested, ... so you just tell her. As long as you know what you are going to say it will be fine.
LES:	But what **am** I going to say?
ALEX:	I thought we'd agreed that.

4

LES:	Anyway, ... who says I'm going to say it? I haven't agreed yet. *(PAUSE.)* When do you think we should do it?
ALEX:	During break-time. I've noticed that she is often on her own then. We can wait until we're sure that no one else can hear and then you can go up to her and tell her.
LES:	But suppose she gets really angry and starts hitting me or something!
ALEX:	No, she won't. She'll probably be glad you've told her.
LES:	I'm not so sure, she can be funny about things.
ALEX:	She's not like that. I **know** she'll be grateful.
LES:	Grateful! That's not how I would feel.
ALEX:	But you're not her.
LES:	Thank goodness! I should hate to be her. Can you imagine?
ALEX:	Dreadful. The sooner we tell her, the better, I think.
LES:	I don't think I can do it. The more I think about it the more difficult it becomes.
ALEX:	Well stop thinking about it then, and just **do** it!
LES:	I wish we had never thought about it. It's none of our business, really.
ALEX:	It **is** our business. And it's important. She needs to know.
LES:	Don't you think that sometimes it's better if people don't know?
ALEX:	No. I don't.
LES:	Really, Alex, I think you can be very hard sometimes ...... you don't think about the way people feel.
ALEX:	Yes I do! That's why it will be so much better coming from you. *(PAUSE.)* She likes you, ... it would only upset her if I told her.

5

LES:	You get out of it all ways. *(PAUSE.)* Alright, I'll tell her ..... but you've got to come with me.
ALEX:	No, that wouldn't work. It would look too obvious. Anyway she'd know we'd been talking about her and we agreed that she shouldn't know that.
LES:	I don't think she'd mind.
ALEX:	We **agreed**, remember? You can't keep changing your mind.
LES:	It's so difficult. The last time I said I'd tell her I spent ages trying to think what to say. And then when I did decide ...... I still couldn't do it.
ALEX:	That's the problem. You think too much, just behave naturally. Talk about something else at first and then you'll find the right moment. Simply say you've been meaning to tell her for some time. She'll understand.
LES:	Well! ..... don't watch. Go away somewhere else and I'll tell you how I got on.
ALEX:	If you insist. *(PAUSE.)* Go on, then.
LES:	Oh, dear!
ALEX:	Good luck.
LES:	I'll need it.

THEY EXIT.

ACTING NOTES

I'm sure you have been in a situation like this and can sympathise with Les. There are very few stage directions here and you are left to decide what the situation is so enjoy this important part of your preparation. You will need to agree with each other and your teacher or director precisely what you have to speak about and then explore how you would feel and behave. You might sit together or move around but you must show how uncomfortable Les becomes and how Alex manages to get out of having to do the difficult job. Ensure that your audience can read this in your faces and movements as well as in your tone of voice. Before you can start rehearsing this scene you need to imagine the conversation that came before so it would be a good idea to improvise this.

COME ON!

Wil and George are on an outdoor expedition and have come to a river which they must cross. The only means of crossing is by balancing on a tree which has fallen across the river. Wil is more confident than George.

THE IMAGINARY TREE TRUNK RUNS ACROSS THE STAGE FROM LEFT TO RIGHT AND GEORGE AND WIL ARE STANDING ON THE BANK OF THE RIVER.

WIL: We've got to cross this river somehow.
(CATCHING SIGHT OF THE FALLEN TREE.)
So we'll use this tree trunk.
(FEELING THE TRUNK WITH A FOOT.)
I think it's strong enough.

GEORGE: I'm not going over there. For a start, it's a very long way down if we fall!

WIL: *(REASSURINGLY.)* We won't fall. It's quite wide.

GEORGE: It looks very slippery.

WIL: Why do you always think of problems?
Just look on the bright side. We'll get across.

GEORGE: Well, you go first and then I'll follow. It's far too narrow for both of us to cross at the same time.

WIL: Alright. Here goes.
(WIL STEPS ON TO THE TREE TRUNK.)
I'll take it very slowly and be careful not to look down.
(BALANCING.)
I'm going to fix my eyes on that tree over there.

WIL ADVANCES SLOWLY WITH ARMS HELD OUT AT THE SIDE AND HEAD UP HIGH

GEORGE: You look like a tight rope walker.

WIL: I feel like one. You know, like those people who used to walk between two skyscrapers in New York!

GEORGE: I wish I was that confident. You're nearly there.

WIL: All you have to do is put one foot in front of the other and you'll get there easily.
(STEPPING OFF THE TRUNK ONTO THE BANK.)
Done it! OK, it's your turn.

7

*FROM THIS POINT ONWARDS THEY CALL ACROSS THE
RIVER TO EACH OTHER. GEORGE IS GROWING VERY
NERVOUS AND MOVES WITH GREAT DIFFICULTY*

GEORGE: I don't like the look of this at all!

WIL: Come on now, just take your time. Put one foot on the trunk and you'll feel how firm it is.

GEORGE: I don't like looking ahead. I think I'll move sideways. I can balance better.
(PAINFULLY TURNING SIDEWAYS, SWAYING MORE AND MORE AND STRUGGLING TO BALANCE.)

WIL: Are you sure that's a good idea?

GEORGE: *(WOBBLING ABOUT.)* Aaaaaa ...... ggh ..... this is horrible! I can feel myself swaying all over the place.

WIL: Come on. Move your left foot. No, more than that!

GEORGE: *(TOO TERRIFIED TO MOVE.)* I can't! ...... my foot is stuck. It won't move.

WIL: Yes it will. Just put all your weight on your right foot for a moment and then move your left.

GEORGE: I can't think which foot is which, you're confusing me.

WIL: *(GETTING VERY IRRITATED.)* You're hopeless.
(TRYING TO BE PATIENT.) Look! gradually edge your foot around until you're facing me.
Come on, you can do it.

GEORGE GRADUALLY MANAGES TO ACCOMPLISH THIS

GEORGE: Ooo ..... eer.

WIL: Right! Now hold your arms out to the side. That's it. *(PAUSE.)* Now come towards me. That's it!
(PAUSE.) Slowly, slowly. You're getting there.

GEORGE: Oh! I wish the wind would stop blowing.

WIL: Don't worry about the wind. It's not that bad. Are you OK?

GEORGE: *(QUIETLY THROUGH GRITTED TEETH.)* Yes.

WIIL:	I can't hear you.
GEORGE:	*(THROUGH TEETH.)* Yeeeesss.
WIL:	Why are you talking in that strange way? Open your mouth.
GEORGE:	I can't! My teeth are stuck together.
WIIL:	You're nearly there. That's it. Come on ...... *(REACHING OUT A HAND.)* take hold of my hand .... one more step. That's it! Well done! You've made it!
GEORGE:	*(COLLAPSING WITH RELIEF.)* Phew! That was terrible! I was terrified. I'm finished. I haven't an ounce of energy left.
WIL:	Let's have a bar of chocolate.
GEORGE:	Good idea! Where is it?
WIL:	In your rucksack.
GEORGE:	In my .... *(SUDDENLY REALISING THAT THE RUCKSACK HAS BEEN LEFT ON THE OTHER BANK.)* ...... I don't believe it! *(LOOKING HELPLESSLY AT THE RUCKSACK IN THE DISTANCE.)* I ...... I left it behind.
WIL:	Oh no! This can't be happening! It can't be for real!

THEY REMAIN STILL AND GLARE AT EACH OTHER

ACTING NOTES

This is a good example of a scene where many of the stage directions are really in the dialogue therefore you must read what each character says very carefully so that you can work out what is happening. You will need a couple of rucksacks for this scene and remember that George must leave a rucksack behind before starting to cross the river. Work hard at the idea of balancing on a narrow tree trunk and take a great deal of time crossing over the river, quite literally, every step is important. Be sure to establish the exact position of the river on the stage.

9

I CAN'T HEAR YOU! - TOGETHER NOW

Biz and Boz are two clowns who have become separated by a sheet of glass. The scene opens as they run towards each other from either side of the stage and collide with the glass.

BIZ:]   *(SPEAKING TOGETHER.)* Ow!
BOZ:]   *(SPEAKING TOGETHER.)* Ouch!

THEY RUB THEIR NOSES AT PRECISELY THE SAME TIME

BIZ:]   *(SPEAKING TOGETHER.)* There's glass. I didn't see it.
BOZ:]   *(SPEAKING TOGETHER.)* There's glass. I didn't see it.

THEY PAUSE THOUGHTFULLY

BIZ:]   *(SPEAKING TOGETHER.)* Can you hear me?
BOZ:]   *(SPEAKING TOGETHER.)* Can you hear me?

BIZ: This is hopeless.

BOZ: This is very difficult.

BIZ: Perhaps I should try shouting.
         (SHOUTING.) Can you hear me?

BOZ: I can't hear you. You'll have to shout!

BIZ: What? I can see your lips moving but I can't hear you!

BOZ: What? I can see that you are moving your lips but I can't hear you!

BIZ: *(POINTING TO EYES AND LIPS.)* Watch my lips. Watch my lips!

BOZ: I can see that you are pointing to your lips. What's the matter with them? Are they sore or are you thirsty?

BIZ: It's no good talking. I can't hear you.
         (POINTING TO EYES.) You've got to watch.

BOZ: Oh! So you've got something in your eye. Well! I can't do anything about that! There's a wall of glass between us! and it seems to stretch right across the room.

BOZ LOOKS AROUND IN PUZZLED FASHION WHILE BIZ IS BUSILY TRYING TO ATTRACT BOZ'S ATTENTION

BOZ:	This is the House of Mirrors. They call this the House of Mirrors. I don't know what's happened. I don't know how we got lost in here. Once we were inside we got lost quite suddenly. It's a trick I think!
BIZ:	If only you would stop talking and just watch we could communicate. *(MOUTHING EVERY SOUND.)* Let's talk very slowly. Let's ..... talk ...... verrry ..... sssslooowlyy.
BOZ:	*(WATCHING INTENTLY AND IMITATING.)* Let's talk verrryy slooowlyyyy.
BIZ:] BOZ:]	*(TRIUMPHANTLY TOGETHER.)* Let's talk very slowly! *(TRIUMPHANTLY TOGETHER.)* Let's talk very slowly!
	THEY BOTH SMILE WITH SATISFACTION
BIZ:] BOZ:]	*(POINTING TOGETHER AT SELF.)* I'll go first. *(POINTING TOGETHER AT BIZ.)* You go first.
BIZ:	*(SLOWLY AND DELIBERATELY.)* How do we get out of here?
BOZ:	*(SLOWLY.)* I don't know. *(FORGETTING TO SPEAK SLOWLY.)* I thought there was a door but every time I turn around I see a reflection of myself and when I look towards you, all I can see is you.
BIZ:	Speak **slooooowly**.
BOZ:	Sorry! I forgot. *(SPEAKING VERY SLOWLY.)* Ssorrry, I ffforgottt.
BIZ:	*(QUICKLY.)* Talk about forget! The trouble with you is that you forget everything we decide.
BOZ:	Pardon? Speeeak slooowlyy. I can't read your lips if you speak so fast.
BIZ:	*(VERY SLOWLY AND LOUDLY.)* Sorrrryy. I ffforgottt.
BOZ:	*(SHOUTING.)* There's no need to shout!
BIZ:	I heard you.
BOZ:	I heard you, too!
BIZ:	That's weird.

11

BOZ:	Perhaps we just imagined ....
BIZ:	No. I heard you ...... clearly.
BOZ:	Where's the glass? *(FEELING FOR THE GLASS.)*
BIZ:	I can touch you. *(HOLDING UP A HAND.)*
BOZ:	I can touch you, too.

THEY HOLD UP THEIR HANDS PALMS TOGETHER FLAT

BIZ:	Did we imagine the glass?
BOZ:	I don't think so ......
BIZ:	The glass ..... was here ..... between us.
BOZ:	Look around the room ...... it's all mirrors now. That's my reflection.

THEY POINT AT DIFFERENT IMAGINARY MIRRORS

BIZ:	And that's mine.
BOZ:]	*(POINTING AT BIZ..)* And that's you.
BIZ:]	*(POINTING AT BOZ..)* .... And that's you.
BOZ:]	*(TOGETHER.)* And there's the door I came in by ......
BIZ:]	*(TOGETHER.)* .... And there's the door I came in by ....
BOZ:]	*(TOGETHER.)* See you outside!
BIZ:]	*(TOGETHER.)* See you outside!

THEY RUN OFF IN OPPOSITE DIRECTIONS

THEY EXIT.

ACTING NOTES

Here is a wonderful opportunity to use your mime skills and also to enjoy the very careful shaping of words when characters are lip reading. You might like to imagine that this scene is set in a fairground but equally this could be a joke that the characters have created for themselves. Work hard to create the illusion of the glass surface. Obviously you must give very careful thought as to where the glass is situated and then decide the precise moment at which they can actually hear each other.

IT DOESN'T MATTER

Rob has recently taken part in auditions for an end of term show and is now sitting alone, centre stage. Gil enters.

GIL: Hi, Rob!

ROB: *(HARDLY LOOKING UP.)* **Oh!** Hi!

GIL: You seem very quiet. What's up?

ROB: It doesn't matter.

GIL: Well, of course it matters. I'm supposed to be your friend, aren't I?

ROB: *(TRYING TO LOOK GRATEFUL)* Yes, you are ...... but it's nothing you can help with. *(PAUSE.)* Really.

GIL: You could tell me about it. *(SITTING.)*

ROB: *(TURNING AWAY OR STANDING.)* No, ... it's stupid. There's no point.

GIL: Please yourself. I just don't like seeing you so miserable.

ROB: *(TURNING BACK.)* Yes. I'm sorry. It's just that I'm so disappointed.

GIL: So, you are going to tell me?

ROB: Well, it's only about the show ...... the end of term show. We've just been told what parts we've been given.

GIL: And?

ROB: I **really** wanted the part of Flick. I know I could have done it and quite a few others said that, too. But I didn't get it.

GIL: That's a pity, did you have auditions?

ROB: Well, sort of, but they didn't really give me a chance to show what I can do. And then, they just pinned up a notice saying what parts we'd been given. I really did hope I could show them what I'm capable of.

GIL:	I thought they knew.
ROB:	They obviously didn't think I was good enough.
GIL:	I don't suppose it was that. You're good enough. It's just that they thought someone else was more suitable. That doesn't mean they didn't think you **could** do it.
ROB:	Oh, I don't know. It's my fault for being so enthusiastic. I ought to be more like the others ..... they don't seem to care what they do.
GIL:	You don't know that! They may be secretly thinking exactly the same as you. Perhaps they've had lots of disappointments.
ROB:	*(PAUSING.)* Perhaps.
	PAUSE
GIL:	So, who did get the part you wanted?
ROB:	Ali, she always does. They seem to pick her every time. I bet it's because her Mum would kick up such a fuss if they didn't!
GIL:	Do you think so?
ROB:	Oh yes, she's always sucking up to them. It's not Ali's fault ...... she's quite nice. She can't help her parents!
GIL:	None of us can.
ROB:	Anyway, it doesn't matter now. She's got the part and I must get on with learning mine.
GIL:	Yes, you didn't tell me what part you did get.
ROB:	Buzz, the character's called Buzz.
GIL:	Who or what's that?
ROB:	It's ...... it's ...... it's the main part, actually.
	PAUSE

GIL:	It's **what?**
ROB:	*(LOOKING CONCERNED.)* What's the matter?
GIL:	*(TURNING AWAY.)* It doesn't matter!

ACTING NOTES

This simple scene contains a situation that is probably familiar to you in some form or other. Concentrate on the small shifts of mood between the two friends. There are a few suggestions for pauses and movements but on the whole these should come from your understanding of the text and the situation. It takes some time for Gil to prize out of Rob what is so upsetting and don't forget that Rob will be very reluctant to agree with anything that Gil may say.

MOBILE PHONES

The two characters A and B may be of either sex and you may decide their names. They have met in a cafeteria and A is carrying drinks to the table. They both have mobile phones and these ring constantly throughout their conversation.

A: *(SITTING DOWN WITH DRINKS.)* It's really good to see you again.

B: And you. *(DRINKING.)* That's better. I was seriously thirsty.

A: So was I! *(DRINKING.)* How are you?

B'S MOBILE RINGS

B: Sorry! That's my mobile.
(TO PHONE.) Hello. ...... Oh! Hi! Yes, I'm sitting with him/her now.
(TO A.) Sam says 'Hi!'

A: Say 'Hi' back.

B: A says 'Hi'. Yes, yes he/she ...... he/she would.

A'S MOBILE RINGS

A: Sorry, that's my phone.
(ANSWERS IT.) Hello.

A:] *(SPEAKING AT THE SAME TIME.)* Really!
B:] Really!

B: When will you be there?

A: I'm on my way now but I just met up with B.
(TO B.) John says 'Hi'.

B: *(TO A.)* Say 'Hi' back.
(TO PHONE.) No. ...... I was talking to A.

A: *(TO PHONE.)* I don't know exactly, about six I should think.

B: *(TO PHONE.)* There isn't a problem ..... just wait till I arrive. ..... Who?

A: *(TO PHONE.)* I will, if I can.

B: *(TO PHONE.)* Why?

A: *(TO PHONE.)* I shouldn't think so.

B: *(TO PHONE.)* OK. Right! See you.
(PUTS PHONE DOWN.)

A: *(TO PHONE.)* Don't worry! Bye.
(PUTS PHONE DOWN.)

B: Sorry about that.

A: No. I'm sorry.

B: So. How are things?

A'S MOBILE RINGS AGAIN

A: Oh, sorry.
(TO PHONE.) Hello. ...... Yes. ...... You're kidding! ..... Well! Don't let him. ..... He shouldn't be allowed to get away with it. I told you what I think about that blue top. ...... No, ... the other one. ..... Alright, alright. ..... Later. ...... Byeeeeee.
(PUTS PHONE DOWN.)
(TO B.) **Honestly!**

B: Problems?

A: No, not really *(SHRUGGING.)* just useless people.

B: Oh dear.
(PAUSE.) Do you want another drink?

A: Thanks, that would be ....

B'S MOBILE RINGS AGAIN

B: Oh! Sorry.
(PICKS UP PHONE)

A: OK, I'll get them.

A GOES OFF TO BUY DRINKS

B: Hello. ...... No. I've **just** met up with A. ...... Yes, fine. Where are you? I thought so ..... there's an awful lot of noise going on your end, I can hardly hear you. ..... I don't know, do I?

A RETURNS AND PUTS DOWN THE DRINKS

B: *(TO A.)* Oh, thanks.
(TO PHONE.) No, I was talking to A. You know ...... that place by the bus station. ..... Yes, ... probably tomorrow. I'll be seeing you later anyway. .... Bring them. OK ......
thanks. ...... See you!
(PUTS PHONE DOWN.)
(TO A.) She's mad.

A: Who?

B: Caroline.

A: She always was.

B: She won't change.

A: *(LOOKING AT WATCH.)* Gosh! Look at the time.

B: I hadn't noticed.

A: I must dash.

THEY BOTH GET UP TO LEAVE

A: It's been really great seeing you.

B: And you. We mustn't leave it so long next time.

A: No.
(LEAVING.) Take care!

B: *(LEAVING.)* See you!

A: *(OVER THE SHOULDER.)* Byeeeeee!

THEY EXIT.

ACTING NOTES

This scene is based on something which actually happened to me and anyone who is interested in communication ought to be worried by the way in which technology has invaded our lives. Note that their telephone conversations are utterly trivial and unnecessary. Try to capture the sense of growing frustration between the two characters but at the same time show the body language of two people who enjoy speaking on mobile phones and letting everyone else know that they do! One of your main decisions will be about how the character **not** speaking on the phone is reacting. Ensure that all the details are accurate even if you have to imagine the phone rings but obviously the scene will be much more effective if you can provide an 'effects' tape.

PILGRIM

This scene is adapted from the great allegory *'The Pilgrim's Progress'*, completed by John Bunyan in 1677. The characters have names which describe their nature and Christian has been told to make a journey to the Celestial City because the city where he lives is to be destroyed. He encounters great difficulties along the way and in this scene Obstinate has just left and Christian is now travelling with Pliable. They are walking along together and Christian has a great pack on his back and carries a book.

CHRISTIAN: Well now, neighbour Pliable, how are you doing? I'm so glad you decided to come along with me. If only Obstinate had known what I can see for the future, he wouldn't have turned back so soon.

PLIABLE: Come, then, neighbour Christian, since there are now only the two of us. Tell me about the things that we shall enjoy in the place we are making for.

CHRISTIAN: I find it easier to **think** of these things than to put them into words ...... but as you are so anxious to know, I'll read about them to you from my book.

PLIABLE: And do you think that the words of your book are certainly true?

CHRISTIAN: Yes, absolutely. It was written by Him that cannot lie.

PLIABLE: Well said! So what things are they?

CHRISTIAN: There is an endless kingdom for us to live in, and everlasting life to be given to us, so that we may inhabit that kingdom for ever.

PLIABLE: *(STOPPING AND WITH GREAT ENTHUSIASM.)* Well said, indeed, and what else?

CHRISTIAN: *(CONTINUING TO REFER TO THE BOOK.)* There are crowns of glory to be given to us and rich clothes that will make us shine like the sun.

PLIABLE: This is very pleasant. And what else?

CHRISTIAN: There will be no more crying or sadness. The owner of this place will wipe away all tears.

PLIABLE: And who else will be there?

CHRISTIAN:	We shall be there …… with angels that will dazzle your eyes, and we shall meet with ten thousand who have gone before us to that place.
PLIABLE:	This all sounds wonderful but how can we share in all of this?
CHRISTIAN:	The Lord, who is Governor of that country, has also recorded that in this book. *(SCANNING THE BOOK.)* Put simply, it says that if you are truly willing to have all these things then the Lord will give them to us freely.
PLIABLE:	Well, my good companion, I'm delighted to hear all these things. So, come on, let's go quicker!
CHRISTIAN:	*(TRYING TO KEEP UP WITH PLIABLE.)* I cannot go as fast as I would wish because of this great pack on my back.
	THEY ARE GRADUALLY SINKING INTO DEEP MUD FROM THIS POINT ONWARDS
PLIABLE:	Watch out. I'm sinking!
CHRISTIAN:	This mud is terrible, I can't lift my feet.
	THEY HAVE BECOME SEPARATED AND CHRISTIAN IS NOW SOME DISTANCE AWAY
PLIABLE:	*(SHOUTING.)* I can only just about move. Help me! This stuff's suffocating me! I'm being smothered by it.
CHRISTIAN:	This must be the Slough of Despond. I can feel myself sinking further, ….. this heavy pack is making me sink quicker.
PLIABLE:	*(FLOUNDERING.)* Ah! neighbour Christian, what has happened to us?
CHRISTIAN:	Truly, I do not know.
PLIABLE:	*(ANGRILY.)* Is this the happiness you told me about? If we make so little progress at the start of our journey, what are we to expect between here and our journey's end? If I can get out of here alive you can go and live in that promised land on your own!
CHRISTIAN:	Pliable. Help me! Stay with me. Don't go.

PLIABLE STRUGGLES OUT OF THE MUD AT THE EXACT
POINT THEY HAD ENTERED EARLIER

PLIABLE: I'm not staying here, I'm going back.

CHRISTIAN: Well, you go. I'm going to struggle on. I'll get out of here somehow.

EXIT PLIABLE.

CHRISTIAN: *(TO SELF.)* If only I didn't have this burden on my back I could pull myself out. ...... I must. **I must.**

ACTING NOTES

There was a time when almost every young person in the English speaking world would have known and read '*The Pilgrim's Progress*' and you should certainly attempt to read the original before tackling this scene. If you are uncertain of the meaning of the word *pliable* be sure to consult a dictionary. We would probably now call the 'Slough of Despond', the 'Swamp of Despair' and it is important that you work very carefully at the moments in which the two characters fall into the soft mud. Do not be put off by what may seem rather old-fashioned language: it has been slightly modernised for this scene and once you appreciate the vivid richness of the words you will find that it works perfectly well as dialogue.

N.B. Although Christian and Pliable were both male in the original text the characters may be played by performers of either sex.

GILGAMESH

'The Epic of Gilgamesh' is possibly the oldest surviving written story in the world. This journey towards self knowledge has some remarkable similarities to the story of *'Noah'* in the *'Old Testament'.* In this scene, Utnapishtim (abbreviated Utna) has been visited by Gilgamesh (abbreviated Gilga) on his journey to find everlasting life.

UTNA IS SITTING WITH GILGA CENTRE STAGE

UTNA: As for you Gilgamesh, do you really think you can find the everlasting life for which you are searching?

GILGA: You must tell me what I must do.

UTNA: *(STANDING.)* Come, I will put you to the test. All you must do is to resist sleep for six days and seven nights.

GILGA: That is easy.

UTNA: *(TO THE AUDIENCE.)* See, a mist of sleep like soft wool from a fleece is already drifting over him now. *(TO GILGA.)* Look at you now, the strong man who would have everlasting life! The mists of sleep are already drifting over you!

GILGA: *(STRUGGLING TO STAY AWAKE.)* No, no, I am not sleeping. I simply have my eyes closed to rest them.

UTNA: Are you sure you would not prefer to go back to your own land in peace ..... back through the gate through which you came?

GILGA: *(JUMPING UP.)* Indeed not! I can triumph in this simple test. *(MOVING TO STAGE RIGHT.)* I will squat here and in six days time I will still be awake. You can leave me if you wish but come at any time and you will find me awake.

GILGA FALLS FAST ASLEEP

UTNA: *(MOVES FORWARD AND SPEAKS TO THE AUDIENCE.)* All men are deceivers. He will even try to deceive my wife. Therefore I will ask her to bake loaves of bread ..... one each day ..... and I will put these beside his head ..... and make a mark on the wall to count the number of days he has slept.

DURING THE ENSUING SILENCE UTNA BRINGS SIX LOAVES AND PLACES THEM ONE AT A TIME BY GILGA'S HEAD AND MAKES A MARK ON THE IMAGINARY WALL.

UTNA: *(SHAKING GILGA.)* Now wake up, Gilgamesh! Wake up!

GILGA: Ah, Utnapishtim. I had barely dosed off when you touched me!

UTNA: Gilgamesh, count these loaves to learn how many days you slept.

GILGA: *(LOOKING AROUND IN A CONFUSED STATE.)* Loaves?

UTNA: These are the loaves my wife baked while you slept.

GILGA: Surely not?

UTNA: One for each day. Look at them!

GILGA: *(FEELING THE LOAVES WITH DISBELIEF.)* The first is very hard.

UTNA: *(TOUCHING THE LOAVES.)* The second is like leather.

GILGA: And the third is soggy.

UTNA: And look here! The crust of this fourth loaf has mould on it.

GILGA: The fifth is mildewed.

UTNA: At least the sixth is fresh. What does that tell you?

GILGA: *(DISPIRITED)* And I fear that the seventh loaf was still over the glowing embers when you touched and woke me.

UTNA: Certainly, it was.

GILGA: So, have I really slept while all these loaves were baked and then became inedible?

UTNA: *(BARELY NODDING.)* Every one of them!

GILGA STANDS WEARILY AND FACES UTNA

GILGA:	*(DESPERATELY.)* What shall I do, 0, Utnapishtim? Where shall I go? I already feel as if some thief in the night is holding my limbs. I seem to have found death instead of finding life!
UTNA:	Who brought you to me in the first place?
GILGA:	0, Utnapishtim, it was Urshanabi, the ferry man, across the waves of the ocean. He brought me to the place where the sun goes down behind the mountain. He told me that, of all people, you were the one to whom the gods have given the secret of everlasting life.
UTNA:	So why were your cheeks so drawn and why was your face so weary?
GILGA:	Why not? I am full of despair and on my journey my skin has been burned with heat and frozen with cold.
UTNA:	*(LAYING A GENTLE HAND ON GILGA.)* Then you shall be healed. The ferry man will lead you to the washing place ..... your long hair will be made as clean as snow ..... your skin will shine as the waters carry away all your cares. *(LEADING GILGA STAGE LEFT.)* And on your return to your own city you will be given new clothes which will never wear out. Gilgamesh, you have found what you were seeking because you realised your own weakness.
GILGA:	*(MOVING DOWN CENTRE, SPEAKING WITH WONDER.)* My life is changed. Today, it begins again.

GILGA EXITS.

UTNA WATCHES GILGA LEAVE

ACTING NOTES

This is a myth and your job as actors is to tell the story strongly and simply. You will not be able to present it 'realistically'. In the theatre we often represent the passage of time in a few moments and a long journey by taking a few steps, here the most important thing of all is to convey the main ideas and to ensure that the wonderful language is enjoyed and understood.

N.B. Translations of this ancient epic are available and you should try to read the entire story if at all possible.

NEW WORLD

In the nineteenth century millions of Irish people embarked from the small port of Cobh (pronounced *cove*) in County Cork for a new life in the United States of America. Small boats would take the passengers to the huge liners moored in the bay and in this scene Charlie and Gerry are looking out to sea on a still evening contemplating the fact that they will be sailing the next day. They spend much of the time in silence and they may be leaning on a railing. The 'sea' lies in the direction of the audience.

> *THERE IS A LONG SILENCE BEFORE THE DIALOGUE*
> *BEGINS*

CHARLIE: It's huge, isn't it!

GERRY: Yes, it's a big ship.

CHARLIE: Think of all those people who will be on board tomorrow.

GERRY: Think of us! Are you scared?

CHARLIE: Yes, **very**.

GERRY: We'll be alright.

CHARLIE: I suppose so ..... but to leave all this behind. *(PAUSE.)* All this!

GERRY: I know. I can't imagine going. *(PAUSE.)* I feel this is where we belong.

CHARLIE: We probably always will feel that way ..... but it's no good thinking that, though, is it?

GERRY: No, we can't stay here. No food, no work.

CHARLIE: Mum and Dad can't take any more.

GERRY: You must not let them know.

CHARLIE: What?

GERRY: That we don't want to go.

CHARLIE: Oh, that! I won't tell. They'll never know. It wouldn't be fair. They feel bad enough as it is.

GERRY:	They've worked so hard to get the fare money together for the journey.
CHARLIE:	Tomorrow. Tomorrow we go!
	THERE IS A LONG SILENCE AS THEY LOOK OUT TO SEA
GERRY:	It's so still, here in the bay. The sea's so calm.
CHARLIE:	Almost peaceful. I wish I ..... wish I felt ...... *(PAUSE.)* It is beautiful, though. *(PAUSE.)* And the ship ...... with all those lights.
GERRY:	Those are the cabins.
CHARLIE:	One will be ours. I wonder where?
GERRY:	I don't know! *(PAUSE.)* We have to go out on the small boat moored alongside here. And then climb up.
CHARLIE:	That'll be fun!
GERRY:	Mum won't like it. She'll be terrified going up the ladder.
CHARLIE:	I don't think it's a ladder ..... more like steps.
GERRY:	Well, it will be swaying around, though.
CHARLIE:	I reckon it will.
GERRY:	I hope the sea's calm like this ...... all the way.
CHARLIE:	I doubt it. I heard the Atlantic can be very rough.
GERRY:	Nearly two weeks ...... on a ship!
CHARLIE:	Time to forget home.
	LONG PAUSE AS THEY LOOK FAR OUT TO SEA
GERRY:	No. I won't forget.
CHARLIE:	Well, I won't forget either ..... but I'm not really sorry to be going. How can you be happy when so much has gone wrong?

27

GERRY:	*(PAUSE.)* Like when we had to leave the lodgings.
CHARLIE:	Do you think we'll ever have our very own house?
GERRY:	Oh, yes! And Dad says there's all these people in New York who make you feel welcome. But he'll have to find a job first ..... before we get the house.
CHARLIE:	He wants to work for the railroad. He wants to go to the West.
GERRY:	So do I.
CHARLIE:	Why the West?
GERRY:	Adventure. Out there you can do anything ...... over here you can do nothing. There's space there ..... this place is too crowded. We're all on top of one another ..... you can never be yourself. Life's too dull here, too boring.
CHARLIE:	I just hope you're right. I've felt we haven't been getting anywhere for too long. *(PAUSE.)* What's the use of going to school and being taught how to please God ..... when all you get is disappointment?
GERRY:	In this life, anyway.
CHARLIE:	That's the only life we understand, isn't it?
	THE DIALOGUE QUICKENS
GERRY:	What about heaven?
CHARLIE:	*(TURNING AWAY IMPATIENTLY.)* I don't believe in heaven.
GERRY:	*(SHOCKED.)* Charlie, you can't! You mustn't!
CHARLIE:	*(TURNING TO CONFRONT.)* They just give you all that to keep you quiet! All this stuff about heaven. They know life is hell here so they say, "Wait till you get to heaven." Well, as far as I'm concerned, heaven is Dad with a job and all of us with decent clothes and, and Mum not having to wash other people's clothes and a room of my own and ......

28

GERRY:	*(TRYING TO STOP THE FLOW.)* Charlie!
CHARLIE:	Listen, Gerry. I know when we're being strung along.
GERRY:	*(HESITATING.)* I've, I've never thought of it like that.
CHARLIE:	*(WITH PASSION.)* Well, it's about time you did!
GERRY:	*(TURNING TO MOVE SOME DISTANCE AWAY.)* Alright, alright, don't take it out on me!
	THERE IS A LONG AWKWARD SILENCE BEFORE CHARLIE GOES OVER TO GERRY
CHARLIE:	I'm sorry. *(GERRY GRUNTS.)* But doesn't it all seem hopeless sometimes?
GERRY:	That's why we're going.
CHARLIE:	*(SLOWLY REALISING.)* Tomorrow!
GERRY:	*(SPEAKING VERY SLOWLY.)* Yes, tomorrow. The New World!
CHARLIE:	The New World. I can't wait!
	THEY EMBRACE

ACTING NOTES

This scene requires great sensitivity and you must get right inside the feelings and situation of the characters to make it work. Allow plenty of time for each thought to form itself and keep the focus and concentration at a very high level. There will not be a great deal of physical movement but small shifts of direction and body language are essential. Try to imagine how apprehensive these two characters must feel and recreate the sense of looking out to sea by the direction of your gaze. Use all the pauses marked but also use your own. Work hard towards the climax of the scene and don't be afraid to use real passion as you near the end.

29

LITTLE WOMEN - BEING NEIGHBOURLY

This scene is based on Louisa M. Alcott's famous book *'Little Women'* that tells the story of a family of girls growing up in nineteenth century America. Jo, the most lively member of the household, is anxious to get to know Laurie the boy next door. She is in the street outside and there is snow on the ground.

THE STAGE REPRESENTS BOTH THE STREET AND LAURIE'S BEDROOM WITH A WINDOW THROUGH WHICH LAURIE CAN VIEW THE STREET BELOW.

JO: There he is, poor boy. All alone and sick this dismal day! It's a shame. I'll toss up a snowball, and make him look out, and then say a kind word to him.

JO MAKES AND THROWS A SNOWBALL THAT HITS THE WINDOW. LAURIE GETS UP AND LOOKS OUT OF THE WINDOW INTO THE STREET BELOW

JO: How do you do? Are you sick?

LAURIE: Better, thank you. I've had a horrible cold, and been shut up a week.

JO: I'm sorry. What do you amuse yourself with?

LAURIE: Nothing. It's as dull as a tomb up here.

JO: Don't you read?

LAURIE: Not much. They won't let me.

JO: Can't someone read to you?

LAURIE: Grandpa does, sometimes, but my books don't interest him, and I hate to ask Brooke all the time.

JO: Isn't there some nice girl who would read and amuse you?

LAURIE: Don't know any.

JO: You know me.

SHE LAUGHS AND STOPS

LAURIE: So I do. Will you come, please?

JO: I'm not quiet and nice, but I'll come, if mother will let me. I'll go ask her. Shut that window like a good boy, and wait till I come.

JO DISAPPEARS AND RE-ENTERS AS IF ENTERING THROUGH THE FRONT DOOR. LAURIE IS BUSY TIDYING UP THE ROOM AND COMBING HIS HAIR

LAURIE: *(CALLING DOWNSTAIRS.)* Alright, Brooke, show her up. It's Miss Jo.

JO ENTERS THE ROOM CARRYING A FULL BASKET

JO: Here I am, bag and baggage. Mother sent her love, Meg wanted me to bring some of her blancmange, she makes it very nice ..... and Beth thought her cats would be comforting. I knew you'd shout at them, but I couldn't refuse, she was so anxious to do something.

LAURIE: *(LAUGHING.)* That looks too pretty to eat.

JO: Oh, it isn't anything, only they all feel kindly, and wanted to show it. Put it away for your tea; it's so simple, you can eat it and, being soft it will slip down without hurting your sore throat.
(LOOKING AROUND.) What a cosy room this is!

LAURIE: It might be, if it was kept nice, but the maids are lazy, and I don't know how to make them mind.
It worries me, though.

JO: I'll put it right in two minutes.
(SHE MOVES THINGS AROUND AND TIDIES UP.)
It only needs to have the hearth brushed ..... so, and the things stood straight on the mantelpiece ...... so, and the books put here, and the bottles there, and your sofa turned from the light, and the pillows plumped up a bit. Now, you're fixed.

LAURIE: *(SITTING ON A SOFA.)* How kind you are. Yes, that's what it wanted. Now, please take the big chair, and let me do something to amuse my company.

JO: No, I came to amuse you. Shall I read aloud?

LAURIE: *(POINTING TO THE BOOKS.)* Thank you, I've read all those, and if you don't mind, I'd rather talk.

JO:	Not a bit; I'll talk all day, if only you set me going. Beth says, I never know when to stop.
LAURIE:	Is Beth the rosy one, who stays at home a good deal and sometimes goes out with a little basket?
JO:	Yes, that's Beth.
LAURIE:	And the pretty one is Meg and the curly haired one is Amy, I believe.
JO:	*(AMAZED.)* How did you **find** that out?
LAURIE:	*(EMBARRASSED.)* Why, you see, I often hear you calling to one another, and when I'm alone up here, I can't help looking over at your house, you always seem to be having such good times. I beg your pardon for being so rude, but sometimes you forget to put down the curtain at the window where the flowers are, and when the lamps are lighted it's like looking at a picture, to see the fire, and you all round the table with your mother. Her face is right opposite; I can't help watching it. *(PAUSE.)* I haven't got any mother you know. *(TURNING AWAY.)*
JO:	*(MOVING TOWARDS HIM.)* We'll never draw that curtain any more, and I give you leave to look as much as you like. I just wish, though, instead of peeping, you'd come over and see us. Mother is so splendid, she'd do you heaps of good, and we'd have jolly times. Wouldn't your grandpa let you?
LAURIE:	I think he would, if your mother asked him. He's very kind, though he doesn't look it; and he lets me do what I like pretty much, only he's afraid I might be a bother to strangers.
JO:	*(WITH GREAT ENTHUSIASM.)* We aren't strangers, we are neighbours, and you needn't think you'd be a bother. We **want** to know you and I've been trying to do this ever so long. We haven't been here a great while, you know, but we have got acquainted with all our neighbours but you.

JO SMILES WARMLY AND LAURIE RESPONDS SHYLY

32

ACTING NOTES

I think we could all agree that a scene like this would probably not take place today! But the way to make this scene 'work' is to play it with great sincerity and an understanding that this seemed perfectly normal when it was written. Jo is a wonderfully bubbly and warm character and never does anything half-heartedly. Her behaviour in this scene must contrast with Laurie's comparative shyness. Take trouble to set up the stage so that the various physical parts of the action that are so clearly indicated in the text can be carried out. You really must read the book if you are to make sense of this extract and you should work to develop a soft American accent.

FOOD

Two young people have just missed a train and are now standing impatiently on the station platform. The bare stage represents part of the platform and a row of chairs represents a station seat.

VIC: If you hadn't insisted on eating another biscuit we would have caught that train.

LOU: I'm sorry!

VIC: All you think about is your stomach!

LOU: That's not fair. Just because you can exist on a lettuce leaf ...... or is it 'rocket' these days?

VIC: *(SITTING AND IMMEDIATELY COOL)* I like to eat healthily.

LOU: Healthily! You have about as much nourishment as a caterpillar!

VIC: Listen, talk like that's not going to help us now. We've missed the train by two minutes and the next one isn't for another hour.

LOU: *(GESTURING WITH DESPAIR AND FRUSTRATION.)* That's stupid! It's only fifty odd miles to get home and it's going to take us two and a half hours to get there.

VIC: Well, it's your fault.

LOU: *(SITTING.)* OK! So it's my fault. How many times are you going to remind me? I can't help it if I have to eat. Everyone has to eat.

VIC: Yes, but not everyone has to eat **all the time!**

LOU: *(STANDING AND ONLY HALF LISTENING.)* I'm starving. I could just murder some chips.

VIC: *(STANDING TOO.)* With Kentucky Fried Chicken?

LOU: Oh yes! And tangy sauce.

VIC: And mushy peas?

LOU: Or sausages.

VIC:	*(WITH GROWING SARCASM.)* A Big Mac, perhaps?
LOU:	No! A massive Starburger Cheesy Whopper.
VIC:	Surely, a Burger King Special with French fries?
	PAUSE AS LOU WONDERS IF THIS IS ALL IRONIC
LOU:	Are you mocking me?
VIC:	Me? **Never.** I'd never do that!
LOU:	*(LOOKING AROUND.)* There must be a chocolate machine somewhere.
VIC:	There is, down the far end of the platform.
LOU:	The trouble is, I haven't got any money.
VIC:	Neither have I.
LOU:	That's why I had an extra biscuit, they were free.
VIC:	*(SITTING RATHER SHEEPISHLY.)* I wish you wouldn't keep thinking and talking about food. I'm hungry, too.
LOU:	You see, I knew you were.
VIC:	No, I wasn't. It's you ….. you made me hungry.
LOU:	That's impossible! You can't **make** somebody hungry. Either you are ….. or you're not!
VIC:	No. I have **become** hungry. The effort of listening to you and the stress you have caused me have made me hungry.
LOU:	Stress! Stress? You sound like my sister. She's always talking about stress at work. And my Mum says a certain amount of stress is good for you and that no one talked about stress when she was young.
VIC:	*(STANDING AND PACING UP AND DOWN.)* Well! that doesn't make it any better. I know that I use up energy just listening to the way you talk.
LOU:	No you don't. It's because you keep moving about.

VIC:	You're the one who can't stand still; no wonder you are always hungry! You've walked about half a mile since we got onto this platform.
LOU:	Don't exaggerate.
VIC:	Honestly, you should see yourself, pacing up and down like a caged tiger. Why don't we just sit and wait? We'll conserve energy!
LOU:	*(THEY BOTH SIT.)* Alright then, let's sit quite still. *(LONG SILENCE.)* Is that your stomach rumbling?
VIC:	No, it was yours. Close your eyes.
LOU:	Why?
VIC:	So that you don't look at that ad for the local Chinese Take Away.
LOU:	*(SUDDENLY INTERESTED.)* Where? I love Chinese food.
VIC:	That man coming towards us has got a portion of chips.
LOU:	I can smell them. ..... Oooooh! I wonder if he would give us one?
VIC:	You'd better ask him.
LOU:	I can't.
VIC:	Chicken!
LOU:	Chicken and chips, I could just murder that!
VIC:	You're nuts! Nutty as ......
LOU:	*(GOING INTO ECSTASY.)* I could eat those, too.
VIC:	Fruitcake ...... absolute fruitcake.
LOU:	Stop it, stop it! This is torture.
VIC:	No, just food for thought!

THEY BOTH REMAIN MOTIONLESS

ACTING NOTES

This scene is based on something which really happened to me and also on a story told me by some friends who described how they used to sit very still because they couldn't afford to buy any food! You need to enter into the situation of the two characters totally before you try to act the scene. Consider how frustrated Vic is really feeling and contrast that with the fact that Lou is constantly hungry. Think how infuriated you have felt when you have narrowly missed a train or bus. The space where you find yourself seems so unwelcoming and lacking in comfort. Make full use of silences and small movements to bring these characters to life.

N.B. You might like to use your own food ideas in this text and add or substitute foods.

IS THERE ANYBODY THERE?

THE WISE PERSON IS SITTING QUITE STILL CENTRE STAGE AND THE SEEKER ENTERS.

SEEKER: *(LOOKING AROUND & CALLING.)* Is there anybody there?

PAUSE

WISE PERSON: Yes, I am here.

SEEKER: How do I find you?

WISE PERSON: Follow the sound of my voice. Then enter. *(PAUSE.)* I am here.

SEEKER: *(STILL LOOKING.)* I'm coming.

WISE PERSON: Well, come along. I'm looking forward to seeing you.

SEEKER: It's difficult. ..... I'm not quite sure. *(ARRIVING.)* Ah!

WISE PERSON: What do you mean, Ah?

SEEKER: I'm sorry, ... it's just that ..... you're not quite what I expected.

WISE PERSON: Really! What **did** you expect?

SEEKER: Well, you're very young. I suppose I expected someone ......

WISE PERSON: Older?

SEEKER: Yes. Yes. You see I came here looking for the 'Wise Person' and I rather imagined it would be someone very old ..... perhaps .....

WISE PERSON: With a long beard or very wrinkled?

SEEKER: Something like that.

WISE PERSON: You've been reading too many fables. You can be both wise and young. Well! sit down, now you're here. *(SEEKER SITS.)* I was expecting you.

SEEKER: Were you?

WISE PERSON:	Oh yes. Either you or someone very much like you.
SEEKER:	So! *(PAUSE.)* You know why I'm here?
WISE PERSON:	You are looking for the great Zanahari.
SEEKER:	*(SURPRISED.)* Yes, I am ..... but how did you know?
WISE PERSON:	Many people look for Zanahari and sooner or later end up here, as part of the journey. The Keeper of the Orchard sent you, didn't he?
SEEKER:	*(EVEN MORE SURPRISED.)* Yes, he did. I did what my dream told me. I went through the orchard without touching the fruit and then the Keeper said I was to look for you. *(STANDING.)* Do you think I'll ever get to Zanahari?
WISE PERSON:	Oh, you will see Zanahari eventually, so long as you follow the way. *(STANDING AND GOING OVER TO THE SEEKER.)* Why are you so anxious to see him?
SEEKER:	*(TURNING AWAY.)* Because I'm not strong and I'm not brave and I'm not clever and I was told that Zanahari gives gifts to all who find him ...... and so I've been looking for him *(PAUSE.)* hoping that he might, perhaps, make me strong ......
WISE PERSON:	Or brave, or intelligent?
SEEKER:	Exactly. How did you guess?
WISE PERSON:	That's what most of them are looking for.
SEEKER:	*(MOVING EAGERLY TOWARDS THE WISE PERSON.)* And do they find what they're searching for? Does Zanahari give them these gifts?
WISE PERSON:	Certainly.
SEEKER:	Then I **must** find him. How **do** I find him? Where do I go next?
WISE PERSON:	*(MOVING AS FAR FORWARD AS POSSIBLE.)* Come with me. Look.

SEEKER:	Where are we looking?
WISE PERSON:	Look over there ..... in the far distance. You see that hedge?
SEEKER:	I think I can. You mean that long strip running across the horizon?
WISE PERSON:	That's it. Now that's the start of the next part of your journey.
SEEKER:	What is it?
WISE PERSON:	It's a maze.
SEEKER:	A maze? What kind of maze?
WISE PERSON:	It's a whole mass of neat hedges ..... and you need to get to the centre and out again. In the centre you will find instructions for the final part of your journey.
SEEKER:	But what if I can't find my way?
WISE PERSON:	You will. You will find that it's much easier than you think.
SEEKER:	Can't you come with me?
WISE PERSON:	That's not possible. It wouldn't help.
SEEKER:	But this is all problems and puzzles and tests and trials!
WISE PERSON:	You have to do this on your own ..... or there is no point in trying to get to Zanahari.
SEEKER:	I sometimes think I never will.
WISE PERSON:	You mustn't give up now. You are so near ..... so near.
SEEKER:	What's Zanahari like?
WISE PERSON:	Ah! you must wait to find out. You won't be disappointed.
SEEKER:	*(DISPIRITED AND WEARY.)* I'm tired.

WISE PERSON:	Yes, you must be. Why don't you rest before you go on? There's no hurry. Lie down here.
SEEKER:	*(LYING DOWN BESIDE THE WISE PERSON WHO IS NOW SITTING CROSS-LEGGED.)* Mmm ...... that's better ...... much better.
WISE PERSON:	Close your eyes. Softly, don't screw them up, close your eyes softly. What can you see?
SEEKER:	I can see clouds ...... and cushions. ...... I see magnificent cushions ...... and a bright light .... and .... mmm .... mmmmm ....
WISE PERSON:	You will get there. You will, just be patient!

THEY ARE BOTH TOTALLY STILL AND SILENT

ACTING NOTES

The contrast in attitude of the two characters must be brought out in this scene. The Seeker is always anxious whilst the Wise Person always remains calm and this contrast needs to be shown, particularly in the way you move. This is a fable or legend and the important thing is for you to understand the story and tell it to the audience by your acting.

adapted from a mini musical THE VOYAGE TO ZANAHARI
by Ken Pickering and John Dawson
used with permission

CATS

Two cats who have never met before come face to face in a narrow alley. At first they speak with all the long vowel sounds greatly exaggerated. At other times they almost spit at each other. The cats are simply known as A and B to avoid confusion because they share the name 'Lucky'!

A: Heeeelloooo.

B: Heeeeeelloo.

A: And whoooo are youuuuu?

B: I miiiight ask youuu the same question.

A: All right, my name is ..... Lucky.

B: *(MISCHIEVOUSLY.)* What an uncommon name.
Who gave you that name?

A: There's nothing wrong with **my** name. My human gave it to me because I'm black and humans say that black cats are lucky.

B: No, there's nothing wrong with the name.
In fact that's my name, too!

A: I don't believe it.

B: It is. That's the name I was given by **my** humans.

A: Humans. You've got more than one! Have you?

B: I've got four.

A: Four!

B: Yes. Two adults and two children.

A: How dreadful! You have to share a home with four humans. Is there room for you? Where do you go to get away from them?

B: I come out here.

A: *(SUSPICIOUSLY.)* I've never seen you before.

B: That's because we've only just moved here. Actually, it's the first time they've let me out. They had this silly notion that I had to be kept in for three days or I would get lost.

A: That's pathetic, cats don't get lost.

B: Well, I'm not so sure about that! All I know is that it got very noisy and uncomfortable in there. Humans are so restless ..... always eating, always talking. And they've no imagination ..... they're always watching a screen.

A: Oh, thank goodness I've only got one! My human's perfect for me. She's so very comfortable to sit on and she sleeps quite a lot. She hasn't got anyone to talk to most of the time so she talks to me.

B: Talks to **you**?

A: Yes. What's wrong with that?

B: Nothing, I suppose. But I just can't imagine what it's like to have a human talking to you. Mine shout.
What do you do when your human talks to you?

A: Sometimes I speak, sometimes I purr. Of course, she doesn't actually understand. I can understand her language perfectly but she can't understand mine. *(YAWNING AND STRETCHING.)* We are **so** much more intelligent.

B: There's the famous story about a cat who spoke English all the time ......

A: *(INTERRUPTING.)* Oh! That Puss in Boots really let the side down! Of course we could all speak English if we wanted but we must never let on.
(CONFIDENTIALLY.) Feline is so much more expressive, far fewer words, too!

B: *(STRETCHING AND CURLING.)* We are superior in every way. Watch and see how I can flex my back ......

THE TWO CATS NOW DEMONSTRATE FLEXIBLE MOVEMENTS

A: ...... and curl.

43

B:	...... and move slowly.
A:	...... and pounce.
B:	...... and stay hidden.
A:	...... and relax.
B:	...... and balance.
A:	...... and squeeze through gaps.
B:	...... and sing.

THEY CATERWAUL THEN BOTH SUDDENLY JUMP BACK AND SQUEAL

A: Ow! What's that!!?

B: Some wretched human didn't like our singing!

A: They never do. Why can't they appreciate **real** music?

B: When you think of the terrible row they make with their voices, their radios, their traffic, their televisions, their so-called music. Yet we sing for a minute and they throw cold water over us. Totally unfair!

A: That's humans for you ..... utterly selfish, think the whole world belongs to them. We have to fit in as best we can.

B: So we need to share everything.

A: **Exactly.**

LONG PAUSE IN WHICH THE CATS MOVE SLOWLY AROUND EACH OTHER

B: So, why are you here?

A: This is my territory.

B: **Your** territory!

A: Yes. You shouldn't be here.

B: Well, I **am** here.

A:	I know. But you shouldn't be.
B:	How can it be **your** territory? It's right outside **my** garden.
A:	That's my territory, too!
B:	Well! all that's got to change. You may be called Lucky like me and we can't help human beings being the way they are ..... but you can't share my territory.
A:	You sound just like a human.
B:	Don't insult me.
A:	*(CROUCHING AS IF TO START A FIGHT.)* Well come on, let's settle this now. **Miaow!**
B:	Meeeeeeooooow.
	THEY ROLL AROUND TOGETHER AND EVENTUALLY SEPARATE
A:	That was a waste of time.
B:	You're right ...... we are as badly behaved as the humans!

THEY RUN OFF IN OPPOSITE DIRECTIONS

THEY EXIT.

ACTING NOTES

You can have some tremendous fun with this scene. Be sure to watch some cats before you decide how you will move as they are so much more relaxed than we are. A black leotard or simple costume will help you to believe you are a cat, too. Remember that the cats are very suspicious of each other at first and use all the space available to you. You might like to use chairs to represent the narrow alley and to provide levels for you to jump up and down. Work very hard on your long vowels to create a catlike sound, really work your speech organs to shape the sounds.

TUNNELS

Chris and Dee have been playing in woods when one of them comes across the entrance to an old wartime building by accident. They begin to explore even though they don't really know what they might find.

THE STAGE IS BARE APART FROM A FEW CHAIRS WHICH ARE ARRANGED TO REPRESENT THE TUNNEL.

DEE IS ALREADY INSIDE THE TUNNEL AND CHRIS CANNOT SEE WHERE DEE HAS GONE

CHRIS: Dee, Dee, where are you?

DEE: I'm down here!

CHRIS: Where? *(LOOKING ANXIOUSLY AROUND.)*

DEE: I'm here, down here! Down here!

CHRIS: This is spooky; I can hear your voice but I can't see you.

DEE: Look down! Look!

CHRIS: *(LOOKING DOWN INTO THE TUNNEL)* There you are, I didn't see you down there.

DEE: Come on, come down. There's a tunnel.

CHRIS: No fear!

DEE: Come on, don't be scared. Let's explore.

CHRIS: Where does it lead?

DEE: I don't know. We'll find out ...... we'll have to crawl.

CHRIS: I don't like this. It's so dark. It smells, too.

THEY BEGIN TO MOVE INTO THE TUNNEL TOGETHER

DEE: Well, it's damp but it's not as dark as you think. Once your eyes get used to it.

DEE HURRIES AHEAD LEAVING CHRIS TRAILING BEHIND

CHRIS: Don't go so fast. Wait for me. I'm scared of bumping my head.

DEE:	Just keep your head down. It seems to get easier along this next stretch. I think I can stand up. Yes, the air feels cooler here, too. Come on, you're nearly there.

THEY GRADUALLY BECOME MORE CONFIDENT

CHRIS:	That's better. What is this place do you think? Where does it lead?
DEE:	I don't know. The strange thing is ….. there's a light coming from somewhere.
CHRIS:	*(SUDDENLY STOPPING.)* What's that!? Listen, what's that?

SILENCE

DEE:	*(LISTENING.)* That's water dripping. I said it was damp.
CHRIS:	Are you sure it's just that? Are you sure it's not rats!
DEE:	No. That's the trouble with you. You always think of the worst possible thing.
CHRIS:	No I don't.
DEE:	You **do!** …… always. It doesn't matter what it is or where we are, you always imagine something scary or horrible.
CHRIS:	Well, I'm just cautious.
DEE:	Cautious, is that what you call it?
CHRIS:	Yes. *(PAUSE.)* So, what do we do now?
DEE:	Go on, of course. I want to know where this leads.
CHRIS:	I don't really like this.
DEE:	*(IMITATING CHRIS.)* I don't really like this! Oh, come on Chris, we can't turn back now. I must find out where that light is coming from.
CHRIS:	Well, don't go so fast ….. don't disappear. I'll follow you.
DEE:	You'll have to go a bit carefully here. There seems to be something blocking the way but I think we can just about squeeze through.

CHRIS: It's the root of a tree and it's grown into the tunnel.

DEE: It's OK, you'll manage to get past. The tunnel's clearer now.

CHRIS: We seem to be going round in a sort of circle.

DEE: We are ..... every so often the walls change direction. *(PAUSE.)* I wonder what this place is, or was?

CHRIS: The walls are very cold and feel very hard.

DEE: Ah! Look, you can see where the light is coming in. Up there, look, a hole in the wall near the roof.

CHRIS: That's an oblong ..... it isn't really a hole.

DEE: Holes don't have to be round!

CHRIS: Well, no ..... but ...... this looks like a small window. You can see how thick the walls are, they're enormous.

DEE: There must be another of these holes round the corner, you can see light coming in.

CHRIS: *(SUDDENLY NOTICING SOMETHING.)* Look, over here! Look! Writing on the wall.

DEE: What does it say?

CHRIS: *(PEERING AT THE WRITING AND GRADUALLY READING IT.)* It's very faint. 'P-T-E   ALAN BLACK   1942'

DEE: Ages ago. That's last century! Let me take a look.

CHRIS: What does P-T-E mean? Pertee? Peetee? or Peter?

DEE: Private, you idiot!

CHRIS: Private? Do you mean it was Alan Black's private room?

DEE: No, no. Private is a kind of soldier: an ordinary soldier who isn't an officer. Don't you see, this place must have been used back in the Second World War!

CHRIS: *(SHRUGGING.)* Perhaps it was. What do you think they kept down here, then?

DEE:	Soldiers, I suppose ...... and guns. I reckon they used to fire out of those gaps.
CHRIS:	Do you think anyone knows about this place except us?
DEE:	*(THINKING ALOUD EXCITEDLY.)* You know, I don't suppose they do. This could be our secret place. I didn't even notice the entrance at first and if we covered it up a bit more, no one would ever find it. Come on, let's do it! This could be our den.
CHRIS:	*(UNCERTAINLY.)* Which way is it to the entrance?
DEE:	We came that way.
CHRIS:	I don't think we did.
DEE:	Are you sure?
CHRIS:	Not really.
DEE:	Which way was it then?
CHRIS:	I don't know!
DEE:	It's very dark.
CHRIS:	There must be ghosts!
DEE:	And spiders!
CHRIS:	And rats!
DEE:	I'm scared.
CHRIS:	So am I.

THEY STAND TOGETHER IN SILENCE

ACTING NOTES

Although there are some stage directions in this piece you really need to decide what is happening by reading what the two characters say. Then you must imagine everything that happens before you try to act the scene. Take things very slowly and work on all the details of how you would move, think, and feel if you were in that situation. There is a great difference in character between the two friends so you must show this.

49

WAITING TO GO TO THE BALL

This scene is taken from the opening of a short gothic mystery story by the Reverend Sabine Baring-Gould, a nineteenth-century English clergyman, who is probably now only remembered for his hymns 'Onward Christian Soldiers' and 'Now the Day is Over'. This remarkable man was a very popular author in his day. He had fifteen children and spent his later years as a school master living in an attic room with a pet owl.

THE STAGE REPRESENTS A VICTORIAN PARLOUR FURNISHED WITH CHAIRS AND A COUCH. IT IS EARLY EVENING.

> JULIA IS MOVING RESTLESSLY AROUND THE ROOM WHILE HER AUNT SITS

JULIA: Aunt, I must go to the ball whatever you say!

AUNT: It is not possible, Julia. I cannot conceive how the idea of attending the county ball can have entered your head after poor, young Mister Hattersley's death.

JULIA: But Aunt, Mister Hattersley is no relation of ours.

AUNT: No relation, perhaps. But you know the poor fellow would not have shot himself if it had not been for you.

JULIA: Oh! Aunt Elizabeth, how can you say so; the verdict was that he took his own life when in an unsound condition of mind. How could I help his blowing out his brains, when those brains were deranged?

AUNT: Julia, do not talk like this. If he did go off his head, it was you who upset him first by drawing him on, leading him to believe that you cared for him, then throwing him over when the Honourable James Lawlor appeared on the scene. Now just consider: what will people say if you do go to this assembly?

JULIA: What will they say if I do **not** go? They will immediately set it down to my having cared deeply for James Hattersley. They will even think there was some sort of engagement.

AUNT: I am sure they will not think that. But really, Julia, you were all smiles and encouragement for a while. *(APPROACHING HER.)* Tell me now, did Mister Hattersley propose to you?

JULIA: *(HESITATING AND TURNING AWAY.)* Well! Yes, he did ...... and I refused him.

AUNT: And then he went and shot himself in despair. Julia, you cannot have the face to go to the ball.

JULIA: *(WITH INCREASING DESPERATION.)* Nobody knows that he proposed. And precisely because I do go everyone will conclude that he did not propose, I do not wish it to be supposed that he did.

AUNT: But his family must have known!

JULIA: Aunt, they have enough trouble without their looking in the paper to see who was at the dance.

AUNT: *(IGNORING THE LAST REMARK.)* His terrible death lies at your door, Julia. How can you have the heart ......

JULIA: I don't see it. Of course I am terribly sorry. I'm awfully sorry for his father, but I cannot bring him to life again. Why couldn't he be like Joe Pomeroy when I rejected **him** ..... go and marry one of his landlady's daughters?

AUNT: Now that's another of your delinquencies; you lured on young Pomeroy till he proposed. Then you refused him ..... and the wretched fellow, in a fit of mortified vanity married a girl greatly beneath him in social standing. You may well have wrecked his life and hers as well.

JULIA: *(INDIGNANTLY.)* I cannot throw myself away as a charity to prevent this man or that from doing something foolish!

AUNT: What I complain of, Julia, is that you encouraged young Mister Pomeroy until Mister Hattersley appeared and then you tossed him aside as soon as you came to know Mister Lawlor ......

JULIA: But, Aunt ......

AUNT: Nowadays a girl lays herself at a man's feet if she likes him. "Where do you see a girl like Viola's sister who let concealment, like a worm i' the bud feed on her damask cheek?"

JULIA:	(ALMOST BURSTING WITH FRUSTRATION.) Aunt! I have no wish to be like Viola's sister ..... neither do I want people to think that James Hattersley cared for me or I for him ...... or that he ever proposed to me; so I **shall** go to the ball.
AUNT:	Well, you know my feelings about this dance. I do not approve. I distinctly disapprove I think your going to the ball is in very bad taste ..... poor Mr Hattersley.
JULIA:	Aunt, will you please stop talking of Hattersley! He is buried.

THE LIGHTS BEGIN TO FADE AND FLICKER AND THERE IS THE SOUND OF A COLD WIND AND THE GRADUAL RATTLING OF WINDOWS. THE WIND GROWS LOUDER AS THE CURTAINS AND JULIA'S HAIR AND SHAWL BEGIN TO BLOW AROUND.

JULIA:	(LOOKING DESPERATELY AROUND.) Is the window behind your chair open?
AUNT:	(TOTALLY UNAWARE OF WHAT IS GOING ON.) No. Why do you ask?
JULIA:	There is such a terrible draught.
AUNT:	Draught! I do not feel one. Perhaps the front door is open.
JULIA:	(LOOKING OUT INTO THE ENTRANCE HALL.) It is blowing harder. It's deadly cold. (TRYING TO WRAP HER SHAWL AROUND HERSELF.) I cannot see where it is coming from.
AUNT:	Julia, what is this?

THE SOUND OF THE WIND GROWS EVEN LOUDER AND JULIA'S HAIR STREAMS IN THE WIND. SHE HOLDS HER HEAD. THERE IS THE SUDDEN LOUD REPORT OF A PISTOL SHOT. JULIA SCREAMS AND CLASPS HER HANDS OVER HER EARS AS SHE SINKS INTO A CHAIR. AUNT ELIZABETH RUNS OVER AND TRIES TO REVIVE HER. SHE RINGS FOR A SERVANT.

AUNT: *(CALLING OUT.)* Rogers. Rogers come at once. Julia, what is it? What is the matter?

ACTING NOTES

This is an exciting ghost story so give it plenty of attack. Don't be put off by the 'old fashioned' and rather formal language: if you speak with conviction it is lively and direct. There is a huge generation gap between the characters and Aunt Elizabeth is rather 'proper' and conventional whereas Julia is fun loving and something of a flirt. Contrast Julia's restlessness with Aunt Elizabeth's stillness.

N.B. You can play the scene as if all the sounds and the blowing wind are in Julia's imagination but there is nothing to stop you creating an effects tape if you prefer.

from THE RING OF LEAD
by Ken Pickering
published by I. E. Clark Inc (USA) and J. Garnet Miller Ltd (UK)
used with permission

SNOW WHITE

Snow White's wicked stepmother has discovered that, although she tried to have her killed, she is now living in a cottage in the woods with seven dwarfs. She disguises herself as a witch and comes to find Snow White and meets a young Prince, who is also looking for Snow White, and sends him in the wrong direction.

SNOW WHITE IS INSIDE THE COTTAGE AND THE WITCH IS APPROACHING THE DOOR

WITCH: He, he, he, he, he, he! How convenient, how romantic if Snow White were to be rescued by a handsome Prince! But it won't happen in **this** story.
Now to my plan and Snow White's death.
(WITCH KNOCKS ON THE DOOR.) Is anyone at home?

SNOW WHITE: Who's that?

WITCH: Why don't you open the door and see who it is?

SNOW WHITE: I can't open the door.

WITCH: Why can't you open the door?

SNOW WHITE: I promised that I would not open the door.

WITCH: I'm only a poor old lady ..... I can't possibly do you any harm.

SNOW WHITE: Well, I know you sound kind and I'm not really afraid but, I'm sorry, I made a promise to the dwarfs who look after me and I can't break a promise.

WITCH: *(ASIDE.)* Curse those dwarfs!
(TO SNOW WHITE.) No. I wouldn't want you to break a promise. By the way, my dear, what is your name?

SNOW WHITE: My name is Snow White.

WITCH: Oh! what a pretty name. What a delightful name!

SNOW WHITE: Why, thank you!

WITCH: Well now, Snow White, I've got some lovely things to show you. The sweetest, juiciest, freshest apples you ever saw. Don't you like sweet fruit?

SNOW WHITE:	Oh yes, I do. I haven't tasted anything like that for days.
WITCH:	Then, perhaps you'd like to see them? You didn't promise not to open a window, did you?
SNOW WHITE:	Well ...... no ...... not exactly.
WITCH:	Then, why not treat yourself, my dear? Just take a look out of your window so that you can see what I have for you in my basket.
SNOW WHITE:	But ..... but ..... I have no money to buy anything.
WITCH:	Oh! don't you worry about that, my dear. I'm sure we can come to some arrangement if you like what you see. Just open the window a crack and you'll see my lovely, shining red apples.
SNOW WHITE:	Oh! I'm sure it will be all right if I open this window a little. *(SHE DOES SO AND PEERS OUT.)* **Oh!** ..... er ..... er ...... Hello!
WITCH:	What's the matter, my dear.
SNOW WHITE:	Nothing. Nothing ..... it's just that .....
WITCH:	Yes?
SNOW WHITE:	I didn't expect you to be ..... um ...... quite like ......
WITCH:	Quite so old and ugly you mean, my dear!
SNOW WHITE:	Well ..... no ..... I mean ..... yes, perhaps not quite so old. I'm sorry, you must think I'm very rude.
WITCH:	Not at all, my dear. You see, I don't really worry about my appearance. I leave all that 'beauty' and 'vanity' to you younger people!
SNOW WHITE:	Ah. I see!
WITCH:	So. Now, you just take a look at my wonderful apples. Let's see, this looks like the very best in my basket. Just look at it. Have you ever seen a fruit so beautiful, so succulent? Don't you feel as if you must sink your teeth into its white flesh at once and taste that sweet juice sliding down your throat. Imagine it, Snow White ...... imagine that luscious taste.

SNOW WHITE: It does sound wonderful.

WITCH: Well then. Reach out of the window and I'll pass it to you. Here you are.

THE WITCH PRETENDS TO STRETCH UP AS FAR AS SHE POSSIBLY CAN BUT SNOW WHITE CANNOT QUITE REACH THE APPLE.

Oh, I'm sorry my dear, I can't quite stretch up that far. It's my poor old back, you know. I'm afraid I am growing terribly old and frail.

SNOW WHITE: Never mind. I can easily open the door for a moment and then you can hand it to me.

WITCH: That is so kind of you. There certainly is no need to be afraid of an old woman like me. I wouldn't harm a fly ...... even if I had the strength..

SNOW WHITE: *(OPENING THE DOOR.)* There, that's much easier. It's so very kind of you to let me try one of your apples. You must have known that I love apples. Thank you.

WITCH: You're very welcome, my dear. Now, you take the biggest bite you can manage from this apple.
(GIVING HER THE POISONED APPLE.)

SNOW WHITE: *(EATING THE APPLE.)* Mmmmmm. That's **so** sweet and ..... er, er ..... er, I feel most peculiar. I don't think I can stand up any longer. I feel as though .... My legs have turned to jelly and my head is going around and around. ..... Help me, ... please help me ....
(SHE FALLS.)

WITCH: Help you, indeed. Help you! There is nothing that can be done to help you now. You can lie there until your precious dwarfs come home ...... and then let them see how well they have looked after you!
(AS SHE BEGINS TO LEAVE.) It worked! The deadly poison of hatred worked and there is no antidote except pure love ..... and where's she going to find that here? Ha, ha, ha, ha, ha, ha, ha, ha, ha ..... !

SNOW WHITE REMAINS LIFELESS ON THE GROUND

WITCH EXITS.

ACTING NOTES

A couple of chairs can represent the inside and outside of the cottage so long as you know exactly where you imagine the door and the window to be. It is worth taking great care with some simple costume and accurate 'props' and it is important that you concentrate on the contrasting voices of the two characters. The Witch is very charming when she is speaking to Snow White but be sure to show her evil nature in the words she speaks to herself and to the audience. Throughout the entire scene Snow White must be hesitant and concerned for the old lady. The most difficult moment is when Snow White is gradually feeling the effects of the poisoned apple: don't rush it!

from the play SNOW WHITE AND THE SEVEN DWARFS
by Ken Pickering
published by I. E. Clark Inc USA and J. Garnet Miller Ltd UK
used with permission

THAT KIND OF COUPLE

This is the opening section of a ten minute play by the young American playwright Shawn Telford. Although the stage direction states that the action takes place in a car you may wish to change the location.

> *A COUPLE IS DRIVING AROUND IN A CAR AND THEY ARE SILENT FOR A WHILE*

1:   We're the kind of couple ......

> *THEY ARE QUIET*

2:   We're the kind of couple?

> *THEY ARE QUIET AGAIN*

2:   What kind of couple?

1:   What?

2:   What kind of couple?

1:   What do you mean?

2:   What kind of couple are we?

1:   Us?

2:   Yes.

1:   I don't know.

2:   You just said ......

1:   Said what?

2:   That we were that kind of couple.

1:   What kind of couple?

2:   You didn't say.

1:   I didn't say?

2:   No, you didn't say.

1:	Then what are you talking about?
2:	What you were talking about.
1:	I didn't say.
2:	I know you didn't say.
1:	Then what?
2:	What you were going to say.
1:	I don't know.
2:	You don't know?
1:	No.
2:	Not at all?
1:	Not at all.
2:	Or you just don't want to say?
1:	Say what?
2:	What you were going to say.
1:	I didn't.
2:	I know you didn't but you were about to.
1:	No I wasn't.
2:	Yes you were. You were clearly about to say something. Something that was about us, you said, "We're the kind of couple ...."
1:	I did?
2:	Yes you did. Forget already?
1:	No.
2:	Then what were you going to say?
1:	Now?

NO ANSWER

1:   I was thinking out loud.

2:   Thinking out loud?

1:   Yeah.

2:   Thinking out loud?

1:   Yeah.

2:   Thinking what?

1:   Things ...... stuff, you know!

2:   Incomplete thoughts?

1:   Incomplete?

2:   Yes, you said, "We're the kind of couple that ...... "
That? .... That what?

NO ANSWER

2:   You don't know?

1:   I don't know.

2:   You just said it out loud. Not knowing what you were
going to say?

1:   I guess so. I didn't mean to.

2:   Didn't mean to or don't want to?

1:   Don't want to what?

2:   Tell me.

1:   Don't want to tell you.

2:   Yes.

1:   I would if I knew.

2:   But you don't know?

1: No, I don't.

2: You don't know what you were about to say. You just happened to have an incomplete thought out loud that was completely and totally pointless without its better half.

1: Sometimes I don't know.

2: Don't know?

1: Don't know what I'm going to say until I say it.

2: Until you say it? And before then it's just hanging there in your head unfinished forming itself as it comes out your mouth?

1: Sometimes.

2: Sometimes?

1: Listen, will you quit repeating everything I say. It's like you've got my every little word on trial.

2: On trial?

1: Yes, on trial! See? You did it just there!

2: Just there?

1: **Ha!** Again! See?

2: Sorry.

1: It's like there's some echo in here. Only it's not some normal echo, this echoes back with a vengeance. My own words are out to get me. Little wicked knives. I have to be careful of everything I say ...... or it will come back on me.

2: Sorry.

THEY ARE QUIET

1: I'm sorry.

THEY ARE QUIET

1: You do it all the time.

2: All the time? ...... Oh, sorry.

THEY ARE QUIET

2: Do I really?

1: Not all the time but you do do it. It makes me feel like you don't believe anything I say. You're always questioning me. I want you to trust me.

2: I do believe you.

1: Do you really?

2: Yes I do. So much sometimes ...... I ...... I trust you so much. I cherish your every word because you're always so honest. I know that you mean what you say. You speak from the heart. That's why when you said, or you were about to say, whatever you were, I really wanted to know what you thought. It was, ... it sounded important to me. I only wanted to know ..... but you don't know.

1: I do ...... know.

2: About us?

1: I do.

2: Tell me what do you think?

1: There are several ......

2: In one word.

1: One?

2: Yes, one. As if to say, "We're the kind of couple that ...... blank." And you fill in the blank with one word.

1: Honestly, I was just thinking out loud. I came to a point in that sentence, that thought, where I didn't know the answer, the finish, and I had already said so much. I had already said it. You heard me. And I didn't know where I was going with it.

2:	It doesn't have to be just one word. Maybe a phrase.
1:	I didn't have an answer.
2:	Nothing?
1:	No, not nothing, just not the word, the one word, to describe us. I did not know what to say. Don't even know why I even said it.
2:	Granted you do have a tendency to think out loud but you don't think incomplete thoughts.
1:	I don't?
2:	No, you always know. You just don't want to say. You were in over your head, caught yourself, suddenly about to say it and backed out at the last minute before the final thought, word, whatever was out. Am I right?

NO ANSWER

| 2: | Am I right? |

NO ANSWER

| 2: | We don't have to talk about it anymore. |

THEY ARE QUIET

2:	Hypothetically, let me ask you a question. Hypothetically speaking, ... lets just say that I asked you to describe what kind of couple we are. So, ... what kind of couple are we?
1:	Hypothetically?
2:	No, really. Really hypothetically. What kind of couple are we? Do you consider us to be?
1:	We are ......
2:	Off the top of your head! First thing!
1:	We ......
2:	You're stalling.

1:	I'm thinking.
2:	No thinking. First thing. Top of your head. You should know this.
1:	We're ......
2:	Just answer!

ACTING NOTES

The playwright has given you total freedom to decide the sex and relationship of the two actors so there is no 'correct' interpretation. The most important feature of a scene like this is for you to trace the lines of thought that are going on underneath the dialogue. Each word is either a response to the previous speech or a new thought that has been prompted by the situation. Don't be afraid of the silences: these are often when the characters are doing their thinking. You may prefer to use an American accent but this is not essential.

N.B. The playwright is currently working in North West America but has been based at a theatre in Kentucky.

from a ten minute play THAT KIND OF COUPLE
by Shawn Telford
used with permission

SALES

In this scene a salesperson calls at the house or flat of a tenant. The scene begins with the salesperson ringing the doorbell and the tenant opening the door.

TENANT: Yes?

SALES: Oh, hello. I'm sorry to trouble you but I happen to be in your area and am making a routine call. I wonder if you would mind answering a few questions?

TENANT: You're trying to sell me something.

SALES: *(SMILING.)* No. No, actually we're carrying out a survey on properties in this vicinity and I didn't think you'd want to be left out.

TENANT: *(STARING DOUBTFULLY AND THEN SPEAKING AS IF GIVING A LECTURE.)* Well, I tell you, this area has gone downhill ever since they let students live in number forty-eight ..... so I hope you've noted that in your survey!

SALES: Actually, that sort of thing comes rather outside .....

TENANT: And there's another thing. When are they going to get these street lamps working? It's so dark round here, it's dangerous!

SALES: *(NOT QUITE SURE HOW TO HANDLE THIS.)* Yes, I'm sure it is. So you don't mind answering a few questions?

TENANT: It depends on what they are.

SALES: Very simple questions ...... totally straightforward.

TENANT: *(HESITATING BEFORE MOVING INTO THE HOUSE.)* Well! Come in, come in.

SALES: *(FOLLOWING.)* Thank you.

TENANT: Do sit down. *(SALES SITS.)* Would you like a cup of tea?

SALES: Umm. No, thank you.

TENANT:	*(SITTING OPPOSITE.)* Fire away then.
SALES:	*(CONSULTING A FILE.)* Have you ever thought of having some form of double glazing?
TENANT:	No.
SALES:	*(TAKEN ABACK BY THE ABRUPTNESS OF REPLY.)* Do you want to say any more about that?
TENANT:	No.
SALES:	*(TRYING TO REMAIN UPBEAT.)* What would you say if we were to offer to double glaze your house absolutely free as part of a new sales promotion?
TENANT:	*(WITH ALMOST DEADPAN EXPRESSION.)* I'd say you were mad.
SALES:	*(LAUGHING FEEBLY.)* Really. Why's that?
TENANT:	Because I have already double glazed this house myself at very considerable expense and I am perfectly satisfied with the result ..... but do continue with the questions.
SALES:	*(NOT TOO SURE HOW TO CONTINUE.)* Hmm, I'm not sure if the rest of the questions apply, actually .....
TENANT:	That's a pity.
SALES:	*(THINKING HARD.)* Ah yes! How recently was your property last painted?
TENANT:	Now that will be, umm, two years ago. You see, I had a fancy for this particular shade of green. Do you like it?
SALES:	I'm afraid I can't say I noticed *(PAUSE.)* but I'm sure it's very **nice.**
TENANT:	*(FIXING WITH A LOOK.)* You don't notice very much, do you? I would think that good observation was essential if you are carrying out a survey.
SALES:	My company trains us to concentrate on the questions we have to ask ..... but I'm sure you're right.

66

TENANT:	Ah, yes. Now, have you got all the answers you wanted? What have you discovered so far in your survey?
SALES:	*(MISERABLY.)* That ...... that there are a lot of houses with double glazing around here ..... and nobody is interested in our once in a lifetime offer.
TENANT:	*(WITH AN EXAGGERATED SHOW OF SYMPATHY.)* Oh dear! I **am** sorry. What a pity. The trouble is ...... no one believes you, my friend. Now, come along, how about that cup of tea?
SALES:	Yes, perhaps I'm better at tea-drinking.

SALESPERSON PUTS DOWN FILE AND CLOSES EYES

ACTING NOTES

You will have to decide if the Tenant is really serious all of the time or playing a game with the Salesperson. Try to imagine the situation, the job which the Salesperson obviously does not really wish to be doing and the Tenant's irritation of having someone like that call at the door. The Salesperson has mastered the sales jargon but is hopelessly inflexible if the answers are not what is hoped for so you must try to recreate the awkwardness and humour of the predicament that both characters are in.

YOU CAN'T DO THAT!

Corry and Andy are taking their first trip on an Underground or Metro train. They have managed to board the train as the doors close and are both out of breath. Two rows of chairs represent the inside of the train.

CORRY AND ANDY SIT SIDE BY SIDE FACING THE AUDIENCE

CORRY: We only just squeezed in before the doors closed.

ANDY: You'd think they'd wait! It could be dangerous.

CORRY: It was bad enough coming down the escalators. All those people with luggage! Why don't they stand on one side?

ANDY: The trouble is, this train goes to the airport, so everyone has loads of luggage.

CORRY: Not everyone. Not quite, not us.

ANDY: Maybe not, but look around.
You can hardly move in here.

CORRY: At least we got a seat.

ANDY: You wouldn't in the rush hour!
(PAUSE.) What are you looking at?

CORRY: I'm trying to read that man's newspaper.

ANDY: Oh! I see. Anything interesting?

CORRY: I don't know ..... he won't keep still.

ANDY: *(LOOKING AROUND SLOWLY THEN SPEAKING QUIETLY.)*
Everyone looks very miserable!

CORRY: Well! Wouldn't you if you had to be down here every day? No daylight!

ANDY: I'd hate it. Rattling around in a dark tunnel. I'd feel trapped.

CORRY: I suppose it's quick.
(PAUSE.) Do you know, I've never been on one of these trains before?

68

ANDY: *(AMAZED.)* I thought you had. I could have sworn you said you'd done this before. You must have done! I was relying on you.

CORRY: No, honestly, this is the first time. Anyway, what do you mean, "relying on me"?

ANDY: You know. I haven't been on one before.

CORRY: *(PUZZLED.)* But I thought .... I was relying on you.

ANDY: For what?

CORRY: No wonder you didn't know what to do with your ticket.

ANDY: It's stopping. Not long between stops, is it?

CORRY: It's four stops before we need to get off.

THERE IS A LONG PAUSE AS THE TRAIN STOPS AT THE STATION AND THEN MOVES OFF. ANDY GRADUALLY BECOMES AWARE THAT CORRY IS STARING UP AT A FIXED POINT ABOVE HEAD HEIGHT OVER THE SEAT OPPOSITE

ANDY: What's so interesting up there?

CORRY: I'm looking at a map of the line. Did you notice the name of that last station?

ANDY: Yes.

CORRY: Well, look up there. See the name of the station where we got on? *(POINTING.)* There. *(ANDY NODS.)* Now look at where we've just stopped.

ANDY: *(STRAINING TO FOLLOW.)* Yes.

CORRY: Now, look for the station where we are going.

ANDY: *(WITH ALARM.)* **Oh, no!** We're going the wrong way!

CORRY: *(WITH A SENSE OF PANIC.)* What do we do?

ANDY: Stop the train!

CORRY: You can't do that!

ANDY:	But **you** said this was the right train.
CORRY:	Don't blame me. All we have to do is to get off at the next stop and then go back the other way.
ANDY:	You can't do that!
CORRY:	Yes you can.
ANDY:	*(STANDING AND LOOKING AROUND HOPEFULLY.)* We'll have to ask someone.
CORRY:	*(STANDING.)* There's no one left to ask. We're the last two on the train.

THEY STRAP HANG AND SWAY ABOUT

ANDY:	I knew this would happen. It would have been so much easier by bus.
CORRY:	What! Stuck in all that traffic! If we leap out at the next station we'll just about make it. Quickly, we need to be ready to get out. *(PAUSE.)* **Now!**

THEY STAND READY FACING THE DOOR

ANDY:	It's stopping. We must look for notices.
CORRY:	Right. **Go!**

THEY BOTH LEAP FORWARD

ACTING NOTES

This very simple scene depends on the tension of discovering you are on the wrong train coupled with the anxiety that accompanies doing anything for the first time. Try to picture the inside of the train and set your chairs with a space for the imaginary doors. Don't forget that you are on a moving train throughout the scene and this will affect your balance and posture. Build the tension by taking the scene slowly up to the point where Corry and Andy realise their mistake. Then you can both panic!

WHAT YOU CAN DO WITH FIFTY PENCE

Sharon and Mandy have met for a drink after work and they discuss the high cost of living. This is an extract from a play which is based on the fact that fifty pence a day could transform the lives of children in many parts of the world.

MANDY IS SITTING AT A TABLE AND CALLS OVER TO SHARON WHO IS AT THE BAR OR COUNTER

MANDY: Get us a packet of crisps, too, will you Shaz.?

SHARON: What do you want ..... cheese an' onion or smoky bacon?

MANDY: Don't mind, really.

SHARON: OK! Two smoky bacon, please. That's another pound, then. Oh, Mand, 'ave you got any change? I've only got a fiver.

MANDY: *(RUMMAGING IN BAG AND PURSE.)* Hold on. Should 'ave it somewhere. Oh blimey! These stupid little fives keep falling out in me bag. Jus' coming. Oh no! I've dropped it now!

MANDY DIVES UNDER THE TABLE

SHARON: What you doin', Mand?

MANDY: *(CRAWLING AROUND UNDER THE TABLE.)* I'm sorry, I'm sorry. Cor, it don't 'arf stink down 'ere. It's all sticky.

SHARON: Leave it Mand, it's disgustin'! It's only about 50p I need. Give us yer bag. I'll find it. *(TO BAR.)* Sorry 'bout this. Here we are. *(COUNTS MONEY OUT.)* fifty-five ...... sixty ...... eighty ...... a quid.

MANDY: Me 'air's all untidy now.

SHARON: *(SITTING WITH MANDY AT TABLE.)* No. It looks nice.

MANDY: I dunno.

SHARON: Honest, it suits you like that. When I last saw you it was all frizzy. I like it like you've got it now.

MANDY:	Yeah, well it cost enough, dunnit? Fifteen quid just for a trim down Dayanis.
SHARON:	I know. I can't afford it no more. Jackie does mine at 'ome now.
MANDY:	Don't blame yer.
SHARON:	Anyway, cheers Mand. I ain't seen yer for ages.
MANDY:	Yer, I know.
SHARON:	What you doin' these days, then?
MANDY:	Workin' in British 'Ome Stores. Started at Christmas.
SHARON:	That's nice. What's it like?
MANDY:	Boring. Pay's not bad though.
SHARON:	What d'yer get?
MANDY:	'Bout three-forty an hour.
SHARON:	Three pounds forty! I don't think that's good. I can get more than that for bar work.
MANDY:	Yeah, I know but it ain't regular is it? Anyway ...... you get cheap food where I am. I get this coupon at the start of the week so I get me lunch for a pound.
SHARON:	Yeah, well that's good.
MANDY:	It all 'elps. Me bus fare's two quid a day now, you know.
SHARON:	What, even wiv' one of them cards?
MANDY:	Yeah. It'd be more like three quid if I didn't 'ave one of 'em.
SHARON:	Drink up, Mand. Come on, can I get you another one?
MANDY:	No. This one's on me.
SHARON:	No, don't be stupid, I'll get them.

MANDY: No you won't. You just sit still. What's it to be?

SHARON: Well, if you insist. I'll tell you what. I'll just 'ave a tomato juice with Worcester sauce.

MANDY: Eagh!

SHARON: No. It's really nice. You wanna try it.

MANDY: How much does it cost then?

SHARON: I dunno exactly, 'bout ninety pence, I think.

MANDY: What! Ninety for a litl' glass of that stuff!

SHARON: Cheaper than lager though, ain't it!

MANDY: I should flippin' well 'ope so!

SHARON: Well, are you goin' to get them drinks or not?

MANDY: What's the 'urry then?

SHARON: It's jus' that I'm goin' to me aerobics class this evening and I don't like me drinks sloshing up and down inside me when we're on the joggin'.

MANDY: Into aerobics then, are we? What's this then? Shaping up for summer?

MANDY HEADS FOR THE COUNTER

SHARON: No, no. Jus' trying to get fit.

MANDY: *(CALLING.)* I fancy a Mars bar, Shaz. D'yer want one?

SHARON: No fanks. It raises me blood sugar too quickly.

MANDY: *(COMING OVER WITH NEW DRINKS AND A MARS BAR.)* What's 50p's worf of Mars bar goin' to do to your blood?

SHARON: Honest. You'd be surprised. 'An If you saved up the money from just two Mars bars you could buy a bag of organic carrots, an' they're much better for you.

MANDY:	Huh! 'Ave you seen the price of them organic fings? They're twice the price of ordinary stuff, an' they're all covered in mud! Don't make no sense.
SHARON:	It does if it's better for you, Mand. Our teacher says ......
MANDY:	What teacher?
SHARON:	Me aerobics teacher.
MANDY:	Oh!
SHARON:	She explains everything at the exercise class. You ought to come, Mand, it's good fer a laugh.
MANDY:	Any blokes there?
SHARON:	No. Well, there's one ..... an old geezer.
MANDY:	No, Shaz, you won't get me there. What do yer do, anyway?
SHARON:	Well, you just pay yer three quid at the door. An' the teacher stands up at the front with her music fing, an' she shows yer these exercises an' we foller. It's good fun.
MANDY:	How long does it last?
SHARON:	'Bout an hour.
MANDY:	How many of yer are there?
SHARON:	Oh, I dunno. Sometimes there's about thirty.
MANDY:	Blimey, she's doin' alright then, ain't she?!
SHARON:	Who?
MANDY:	Your teacher. Thirty people all coughing up three quid for an hour. That's ...... *(ATTEMPTING TO COUNT USING HER FINGERS.)* ..... thirty three poundses she gets for just an hour!
SHARON:	Well, yeah. It's hard work though.

MANDY:	Maybe it is, but I wouldn't turn me nose up at earning that much.
SHARON:	I reckon she deserves it. Look, I've got to go, Mand but we oughta meet up again. Why don't yer give me a ring tomorra night when you get in. Actually, you couldn't lend us 20p could yer?
MANDY:	Yeah, sure. I've got plenty of change.
SHARON:	I've gotter make a quick 'phone call.

ACTING NOTES

The play from which this was taken is really a series of short sketches based on a theme so don't be put off by the sudden ending. This kind of dialogue might have come from a play by Mike Leigh and you are free to adapt the accent and some of the details of prices to suit your local accents and knowledge. Although the characters use language in a way which might be considered rather unsophisticated there is a very lively quality in their mode of communication which you must try to capture. Don't exaggerate the 'cockney' or 'non received' pronunciation but base your work on what you actually hear in everyday life. This scene is an accurate account of a conversation between two young women and you will need to think of the attitudes, body language, dress, tone of voice and behaviour of the two characters as well as working out the precise details of the situation.

from ONE CHILD AT A TIME
by Ken Pickering
published by J. Garnet Miller Ltd
used with permission

ADDITIONAL TITLES

All books may be ordered direct from:

DRAMATIC LINES   PO BOX 201   TWICKENHAM   TW2 5RQ
tel: 020 8296 9502   fax: 020 8296 9503

MONOLOGUES

THE SIEVE AND OTHER SCENES
Heather Stephens
ISBN 0 9522224 0 X

The Sieve contains unusual short original monologues valid for junior acting examinations. The material in The Sieve has proved popular with winning entries worldwide in drama festival competitions. Although these monologues were originally written for the 8-14 year age range they have been used by adult actors for audition and performance pieces. Each monologue is seen through the eyes of a young person with varied subject matter including tough social issues such as fear, 'Television Spinechiller', senile dementia, 'Seen Through a Glass Darkly' and withdrawal from the world in 'The Sieve'. Other pieces include: 'A Game of Chicken', 'The Present', 'Balloon Race' and a widely used new adaptation of Hans Christian Andersen's 'The Little Match Girl' in monologue form.

CABBAGE AND OTHER SCENES
Heather Stephens
ISBN 0 9522224 5 0

Following the success of The Sieve, Heather Stephens has written an additional book of monologues with thought provoking and layered subject matter valid for junior acting examinations. The Cabbage monologues were originally written for the 8-14 year age range but have been used by adult actors for audition and performance pieces. The Aberfan slag heap disaster issues are graphically confronted in 'Aberfan Prophecy' and 'The Surviving Twin' whilst humorous perceptions of life are observed by young people in 'The Tap Dancer' and 'Cabbage'. Other pieces include: 'The Dinner Party Guest', 'Nine Lives' and a new adaptation of Robert Browning's 'The Pied Piper' seen through the eyes of the crippled child.

ALONE IN MY ROOM ORIGINAL MONOLOGUES
Ken Pickering
ISBN 0 9537770 0 6

This collection of short original monologues includes extracts from the author's longer works in addition to the classics. Provocative issues such as poverty and land abuse are explored in 'One Child at a Time', 'The Young Person Talks' and 'Turtle Island' with adaptations from 'Jane Eyre', Gulliver's Travels' and 'Oliver Twist' and well loved authors including Dostoyevsky. These monologues have a wide variety of applications including syllabus recommendation for acting examinations. Each monologue has a brief background description and acting notes.

PEARS

Heather Stephens
ISBN 0 9522224 6 9

Heather Stephens has written layered, thought provoking and unusual short original duologues to provide new material for speech and drama festival candidates in the 8-14 year age range. The scenes have also been widely used for junior acting examinations and in a variety of school situations and theatrical applications. Challenging topics in Pears include the emotive issues of child migration, 'Blondie', 'The Outback Institution' and bullying 'Bullies', other scenes examine friendship, 'The Best of Friends', 'The Row' and envy, 'Never the Bridesmaid'. New duologue adaptations of part scenes from the classic play, 'Peace' by Aristophanes and 'Oliver Twist' by Charles Dickens are also included.

SHAKESPEARE THE REWRITES

Claire Jones
ISBN 0 9522224 8 5

A collection of short monologues and duologues for female players. The scenes are from rewrites of Shakespeare plays from 1670 to the present day written by authors seeking to embellish original texts for performances, to add prequels or sequels or to satisfy their own very personal ideas about production. This material is fresh and unusual and will provide exciting new audition and examination material. Comparisons with the original Shakespeare text are fascinating and this book will provide a useful contribution to Theatre Study work from G.CSE to beyond 'A' level. Contributors include James Thurber (Macbeth) Arnold Wesker (Merchant of Venice) and Peter Ustinov (Romanoff and Juliet). The collection also includes a most unusual Japanese version of Hamlet.

JELLY BEANS

Joseph McNair Stover
ISBN 0 9522224 7 7

The distinctive style and deceptively simple logic of American writer Joseph McNair Stover has universal appeal with scenes that vary in tone from whimsical to serious and focus on young peoples relationships in the contemporary world. The collection of 10-15 minute original scenes for 2, 3 and 4 players is suitable for 11 year olds through to adult. Minimal use of sets and props makes pieces ideal for group acting examinations, classroom drama, assemblies and various other theatrical applications and have been used with success at Young Writers Workshops to teach the elements of script writing and dramatic development.

WILL SHAKESPEARE SAVE US!
WILL SHAKESPEARE SAVE THE KING!

Paul Nimmo

ISBN 0 9522224 1 8

Two versatile plays in which famous speeches and scenes from Shakespeare are acted out as part of a comic story about a bored king and his troupe of players.   These plays are suitable for the 11-18 year age range and have been produced with varying ages within the same cast and also performed by adults to a young audience. The plays can be produced as a double bill, alternatively each will stand on its own, performed by a minimum cast of 10 without a set, few props and modern dress or large cast, traditional set and costumes. The scripts are ideal for reading aloud by classes or groups and provide an excellent introduction to the works of Shakespeare. Both plays have been successfully performed on tour and at the Shakespeare's Globe in London.

SUGAR ON SUNDAYS AND OTHER PLAYS

Andrew Gordon

ISBN 0 9522224 3 4

A collection of six one act plays bringing history alive through drama.   History is viewed through the eyes of ordinary people and each play is packed with details about everyday life, important events and developments of the period.   The plays can be used as classroom drama, for school performances and group acting examinations and can also be used as shared texts for the literacy hour. The plays are suitable for children from Key Stage 2 upwards and are 40-50 minutes in length and explore Ancient Egypt, Ancient Greece, Anglo-Saxon and Viking Times, Victorian Britain and the Second World War. A glossary of key words helps to develop children's historical understanding of National Curriculum History Topics and the plays provide opportunities for children to enjoy role play and performance.

LESSONS

DRAMA LESSONS IN ACTION

Antoinette Line

ISBN 0 9522224 2 6

Resource material suitable for classroom and assembly use for teachers of junior and secondary age pupils. Lessons are taught through improvisation. These are not presented as 'model lessons' but provide ideas for adaptation and further development.   The lessons include warm-up and speech exercises and many themes are developed through feelings such as timidity, resentfulness, sensitivity and suspicion. The material can be used by groups of varying sizes and pupils are asked to respond to interesting texts from a diverse selection of well known authors including: Roald Dahl, Ogden Nash, Ted Hughes, Michael Rosen, Oscar Wilde and John Betjeman.

X-STACY
Margery Forde
ISBN 0 9522224 9 3

Margery Forde's powerful play centres on the rave culture and illicit teenage drug use and asks tough questions about family, friends and mutual responsibilities. The play has proved hugely successful in Australia and this English edition is published with extensive teachers' notes by Helen Radian, Lecturer of Drama at Queensland University of Technology, to enrich its value for the secondary school classroom, PSHE studies, English and drama departments.

WHAT IS THE MATTER WITH MARY JANE?
Wendy Harmer
ISBN 0 9522224 4 2

This monodrama about a recovering anorexic and bulimic takes the audience into the painful reality of a young woman afflicted by eating disorders. The play is based on the personal experience of actress Sancia Robinson and has proved hugely popular in Australia. It is written with warmth and extraordinary honesty and the language, humour and style appeal to current youth culture. A study guide for teachers and students by Dianne Mackenzie, Curriculum Officer for English and Drama, New South Wales is included in this English edition ensuring that the material is ideal for use in the secondary school classroom and for PSHE studies, drama departments in schools and colleges in addition to amateur and professional performance.